THE VISIBILITY FORMULA

Taking Your Business From Best Kept Secret to Household Name

NNEKA UNACHUKWU, MD

ENTREMD

The Visibility Formula
Taking Your Business From Best Kept Secret to Household Name

ISBN   Hardcover 978-1-963503-00-5
          Paperback 978-1-963503-01-2
          Ebook 978-1-963503-02-9

To Steve, my husband and coach who inspired me to build an omnipresent brand.

Table of Contents:

Introduction:

Obscurity

This is the number one problem every business has. There are thousands of people right now who have the problem your business solves and they are willing and able to pay for your product or service. They are actively looking for someone just like you. The only reason they are not your client right now is because they have no idea you exist.

One of your most important jobs as an entrepreneur is to put yourself out there loud enough and long enough so the people who desperately need you can find you.
I was a socially awkward, painfully shy, introverted introvert who discovered this the hard way. Now, a decade and half later, I have mastered the art of exponentially increasing my visibility and built three very successful companies.

This book is my way of showing you the shortcut to success. I will break down the strategies, debunk the myths and help you overcome every mental block that will try to stop you. You have in your hand the exact formula that will take you from best kept secret to household name.

The result will be a business that helps so many more clients, creates more financial and time freedom for you and gives you a sense of fulfillment that makes everything worth it.

Nice to Meet You

In case this is your first introduction to me, hi! I'm Dr. Una. The most important thing about me is that I love physicians. I love us. I really do. Fifteen years ago, I finished my pediatric training and got a job like pediatricians do. A little over a year later, my boss told me I should start my own practice, and I thought he was crazy. Nobody starts a practice 15 months out of residency. And then I did it. I started my own practice. I knew I was a good doctor, so why not give it a shot?

I remember setting up shop, thinking everyone would come. I hung up the shingle, and nobody came. I didn't know I was going to need to know how to market. I didn't know I would need to build a referral base. I thought my good intentions, expertise and bedside manner were enough. I thought I was just going to help people and everything else would take care of itself.

Everything else will not take care of itself.

People find it very hard to believe now, but I was a super shy, socially-awkward introverted introvert back then. The thought of doing the things I needed to do to work my business was terrifying. I couldn't imagine getting up in front of people and talking, and I didn't know a single thing about business.

Then I realized that all business skills are learnable.

I went after learning and doing, and I went after it hard. I dared my fears and went all in. Fast forward a few years, and I'm a serial entrepreneur who runs three companies and a non-profit. My favorite company (don't tell the others!) is EntreMD where I help doctors build profitable businesses so they have the freedom to live life and practice medicine on their terms. We founded the EntreMD Business School (EBS), an amazing place for physicians where business dreams come true. We've served over 250 doctors so far. I'm a bestselling author of multiple books and have a podcast with over 600,000 downloads.

It's all such a joy. Seriously. I work hard, but it doesn't feel like work at all. I tell people that, ever since I started EntreMD, I haven't worked a day since. It's too much fun to call it work.

The reason I do everything I do is to be an example, a vision board of sorts, for physicians. I'm here saying, hey guys, don't believe the lie that private practice is dead. Don't believe the lie that physicians can't be entrepreneurs. I'm proof of what is possible for us. And that's the reason I'm writing this book. Because it's possible. And not just for me, but for you too.

Not only do I love doctors, but I believe in us. No matter how crazy it looks, I honestly believe this is the best time to be a physician. Things look bleak, but we're going to turn it all around. My big dream is to help 100,000 physicians build profitable businesses. Why 100k? Because, that number represents ten percent of the physician community. Once we have that number, the whole system is going to topple. Everything will change, because we'll have enough examples of how possible it is.

So you're in a really safe space here. My intention for this book is for you to get so much out of this, and gain so much forward momentum. Maybe more than you've made all year long. That's the idea. We're going to dig in and we're going to get stuff done. And it's going to blow your mind.

What Is the Visibility Formula?

The Visibility Formula Workshop is an event I've hosted several times now where we've helped hundreds of doctors create massive momentum in their businesses. I wanted even more physicians to have access to this incredible experience, so I turned it into a book.

I love the Visibility Formula so much. It's simple. It's something that doctors can implement to own their business and their brand, to 10x their visibility. Because we know that everything starts from visibility. If nobody can find you, they don't know you, and if they don't know you, they can't know, like, and trust you.

And that is the currency for a very successful business.

This book is a blueprint for visibility. I'll show you how to become known for what you do, how to amplify your message, how to find your ideal clients and get them to jump at the opportunity to work with you, and how to build a system so that you can get your time back and have the freedom to live a life you love. We'll talk about building a platform. We'll talk about leaving a legacy to those who come behind you. We'll learn about batching and delegation and repurposing—and so much more.

I want you to treat this book like you paid ten thousand dollars for it. Read it, then implement everything you've learned.

Are You Ready to Grow?

This book is for physicians who have an interest in hyper-growth. It doesn't matter if you're in private practice, direct primary care, direct specialty care, an intrapreneur (working a full-time job)—or a speaker, coach, or consultant in the healthcare industry. This is for you if you want to grow your business, whether that's hitting 6 figures, 7 figures, or multiple 7 figures. Or you're running a business and want to help train your team to pull their own weight for growth. Maybe you want to launch your brand or build it out. Whatever it is you want to do, you know there's more.

Maybe you're thinking, "My goals aren't as grand as all that. Right now I'm just feeling stuck." If you're reading this book because you've tried a lot of things, and nothing's working, and you feel like you hit a brick wall and don't know where to turn, this is the right book for you.

Let me tell you a quick story. The day before the very first EntreMD Live event in 2019, I had a nurse practitioner quit. You can imagine where my mind went. "This means my business is not a place where people want to stay. This means I'm not a good leader. This means I can't maintain company culture. What do I do now?"

I felt stuck. I wanted to quit. I felt like my business just wasn't working how it should be working, so how could I teach other people how to run their businesses? I felt like a fraud, an impostor. This was 2019, and EntreMD was just a little baby, less than six months old. I had the opportunity to work through this and move forward with my current reality—or quit.

I am so grateful that I didn't give in to those feelings, that I didn't quit. EntreMD is now five years old. We've gone on to write books. We have a podcast that's a 1% podcast on a global scale. We have over 600,000 downloads. We've helped hundreds of doctors build successful businesses. We've helped many, many people cross the 6-figure, the 7-figure and multiple 7-figure mark.

We're not quitting.

Being stuck is a temporary problem. It's a problem I've overcome time and time again. I'm here to help you get unstuck. Wherever you are right now in your business, whatever your mindset is, whatever is in the way of you achieving your goals and living your dreams, we're going to get through it. We're moving forward.

It's time to lean in and focus.

We're going to set the intention and be committed to massive transformation. We'll work on our brands, on our businesses, and get them in front of our ideal clients. When you finish this book, if you've done the homework, and you commit to the ongoing work, your business will be different. The transformation will be wild. Not just in your business, but in *you*.

Three Things that Can Stop Us If We Let Them

I get entrepreneurs—their struggles, their challenges, the fears that stop them from living their dreams. I've overcome these very things, so I'm the perfect person to help you overcome them too. Before we get to the meat of the book, we're going to talk about three things that can stop us on the road to our dreams if we let them.

But we're not going to let them.

#1: The status quo

Right here, right now, I want you to decide to reject the status quo, no matter how beautiful it is. I want you to say to yourself: I'm deciding once and for all that this is the last time my business will look the way it looks right now. Because I'm ready to go to the next level. I don't care what it takes. I'm doing it. I don't want to get to the end of my life and say, "Why didn't I follow my dream?"

It's possible that your business looks great. Maybe you're celebrating a 7-figure milestone. So why are you reading this book? Because you want it to be better. You know you need to immerse yourself in as many resources about entrepreneurship as you can.

No matter where you're at in your business, you can always always always uplevel. No more business as usual. No more "this is all I know." No more status quo.

#2: Fear

You are going to have so many opportunities to be afraid. Believe me. Fear is going to show up. It's going to show up *a lot*. We're going to talk about fear a lot in this book. We're going to normalize it so it can't defeat us. This way, when it does show up, you can say, "Oh, I heard about you. I knew you were going to show up. Dr. Una told me all about you."

Why is fear going to show up? Because this is what fear does when you take a big leap. You're reading this book because you want different results. You're here because you want your business to look different. No matter where you are on your entrepreneurial journey, you want to be somewhere different, somewhere better. If you want to be somewhere different, you have to do things that are different. You have to step outside of your comfort zone.

Enter fear.

At the risk of stating the obvious, we are comfortable in our comfort zones. Comfort zones are familiar. They're easy and safe. But the comfort zone is where great dreams go to die. There's nothing magical that happens in the comfort zone. When we get outside of our comfort zone, fear shows up. Every single time.

But fear doesn't mean stop.

Let me say that again. *Fear doesn't mean stop.* This is one of the things that was most revolutionary for me. I used to think fear was a red flag, a stop sign. But that's not what fear means. It just means that you're at the border, the edge, of your comfort zone. You're about to step outside of your comfort zone where all the magic happens. Fear doesn't want you to leave your comfort zone. But it's the only way to get to your dream life.

Once you get comfortable being uncomfortable, the whole world opens up for you. Eventually you will feel excitement when you bump up against discomfort, and be thrilled to face a challenge—even though the fear or discomfort won't ever disappear. I still feel it all these years later.

I don't know about you, but I'm not letting fear get in the way of magic happening. For so long, I was frozen by fear. I was afraid of putting myself out there, afraid of speaking, afraid of owning my business ideas, afraid of owning my voice. And then I had a realization. We're burning daylight here. This is not the dress rehearsal.

This is life. I only get one shot at it.

I'm 44 now. When I turn 90, and I look back at what I could have done at 44, I don't want to have regrets. I'm not saying no to my dreams for one more day because of fear. I want to live the fullest, most beautiful life I possibly can—and then leave an incredible legacy behind me when I go.

I want you to say out loud right now: "Fear is not going to stop me. I only get one shot at this." Own it. We're going to be learning and doing some really great things. And we're not going to let fear get in our way.

#3: Overwhelm, confusion, and perfectionism

Overwhelm, confusion, and perfectionism are fear's cousins. You're going to read so many great things in this book and think, "Oh my goodness, that's amazing." Then overwhelm will show up, and you'll think, "Oh, no. There are so many things. I can't do all of those things."

You're going to feel overwhelmed, then confused. *Where do I start? How do I do this? I can't do this.* Then perfectionism is going to rear its little head. Instead of taking immediate action and doing a video to promote your business, you'll think, "Maybe I should take a six-month course on making videos first." No, we're not going for perfection here. Perfection is an important target if you're a neurosurgeon. It's not required if you want to be an entrepreneur.

You're going to take a deep breath, and just like you're not going to give in to fear, you're not going to give in to overwhelm and confusion and perfectionism. Instead of being overwhelmed, you'll look at the very next thing to do and do that. Then the very next thing. Then the very next thing. You don't have to be overwhelmed. You don't have to be confused. You don't have to be perfect. You're going to take one imperfect action step at a time. Perfection isn't important. Moving forward is.

And speaking of moving forward, let's take a deep breath and dive into the Visibility Formula. This is going to be so much fun.

If you haven't already done so, head over to www.entremd.com/visiblitybook to download your workbook.

CHAPTER 1:

How to Become Known for What You Do

What's the number one problem our businesses have right now? Obscurity.

Our problem is not that our ideal clients don't exist. They exist. They just don't know *we* exist, so they can't find us. If they can't find us, they can't work with us. If they don't work with us, we don't have the opportunity to serve them, and we don't have the opportunity to earn.

You may be saying, "No, Dr. Una, obscurity is not my problem. My problem is that my revenue goal for the year is $1 million. I just need to hit that."

Let's think about this for a minute. One million dollars in revenue is going to come from x number of clients, and x number of clients is going to require you saying "come work with me" for them to come work with you. For you to say "come work with me," you have to put yourself in a position for them to know you, like you, and trust you. For them to know you, like you, and trust you, they have to know you're out there.

It all goes back to obscurity.

One of the most challenging things you'll face in your business is to get your message in front of as many people who need, want, and are willing to pay for your product and service as possible. Our biggest problem really is obscurity.

So that's what we're going to be fixing with the Visibility Formula. We have to find a way to go from invisible to visible. We need eyes on what we do. We have to get in front of people. And not just any people, but people who have a problem that we can solve. We need to amplify our message to create a critical mass of clients that can make our businesses wildly successful.

We have to become known for what we do.

What Do You Do?

Before we talk about becoming known for what we do, it's important that *we know what we do*. Some people come to me with a brilliant business idea fully formed. They just need to know how to amplify their message. But not everyone has a clear idea of what they want to do. They know there's something and it's valuable and important, but all the pieces just haven't clicked in place for them yet. Is that you?

Does it seem like everyone else has a great idea, and you can't find one? You know you want to be an entrepreneur and make a lot of money and have the freedom to live life and practice medicine on your terms, but you don't know exactly what you want to do?

In my book, *The EntreMD Method*, in Chapter 9 "Find Your Idea," I share 5 Questions to Find a Great Business Idea. I explain these in great detail in the book (go buy it and read it if you haven't already), but I'll give you the questions here.

1. What problems have you solved for yourself and others?
2. What skills/certifications do you have?
3. What do you love and would do for free?
4. What can you do faster/cheaper/better?
5. What makes you sad or mad?

I also give you an "Idea Matrix" to filter your dreams through to make sure that your business will serve *and* earn. You have to have both. We're not talking about hobbies here or labors of love. We're building profitable businesses. And I share 23 proven business ideas for physicians that fall under the categories of private practice ideas, personal brand ideas, marketing-based ideas, consulting and coaching ideas, and consumer products.

One of the best ideas you can have is a business that helps people with a problem that you've already overcome. What problem did you once have that you have since solved and are now perfectly equipped to help others solve that exact problem? I help physicians start businesses that help them live life and practice medicine on their terms because that's what I did.

After you have an idea, you have to craft a message. People want to know "what's in it for me?" and your messaging has to answer that question. Otherwise they won't care. They care about themselves and the problem they have and finding someone who can solve it.

Once you have your business idea—and it can absolutely evolve over time as most good ideas do—then you can get to work on becoming known for what you do.

How Do I Become the Go-To Person in My Area of Expertise?

When I started my very first business—my private practice—14 years ago, I remember wondering how I was going to fill up my schedule and get all the patients I wanted. Then I heard Brian Tracy say that 80% of the people who have the problem you solve are *aware* that they have the problem and they want to *solve* the problem, and they're willing and able to *pay* for it, they would *love* to work with you, but they have no idea you exist.

We have to become known for what we do.

This is what we want. When someone in our industry thinks of an expert in that industry, we want them to think of us first. We want to be top of mind. When someone thinks of an allergist, they think of you. When they think about weight loss, they think of you. When they think of relief from fibromyalgia, they think of you. When they think about fixing infertility, they think about you. When they think about speakers in your area of expertise, they think about you.

How do you become known for what you do?

The things I'm going to share with you in this chapter are simple, but profound. The problem with simple things is that they're easy to do, and they're easy *not* to do. Whenever I share a simple, timeless strategy and someone says, "I already knew about that," my question is this: "But are you doing it?" More often than not, their answer is a sheepish no. We're going to choose to do it. We're going to take action.

The person I first heard talk about this concept of becoming known for what you do is a man named Rory Vaden (you can watch his YouTube videos) and he heard it from Peter Sheahan. The concept is called Sheahan's Wall. On one side of the wall are all the businesses that are *unknown*. On the other side of the wall are the few businesses that are *known*.

Think about the NBA for example. You have the players everyone knows. Then there are the players that don't play much and people don't know them. The known players are on one side of Sheahan's Wall, and the unknown players are on the other.

Right now, most likely, you're on the unknown side of the wall. If you want to become known for what you do, you have to find a way to break through to the other side. The wall is too tall to climb, so you have to go through it with a hammer.

There are two different methods you can use. You can take your hammer and just start hitting the wall all over the place. But it's a really strong wall, a really thick wall, so you end up using all of your energy and scattering your effort. And you barely made a dent, let alone busted through to the other side.

The wall is never coming down that way.

The other tactic you can try is to keep hitting in one spot over and over again. Over and over and over and over again. If you do this consistently, day in and day out, it's only a matter of time until you break through and come out on the other side.

If you want to be known for what you do, the price for that is focused effort. Consistent focused effort over time.

You Have to Own One Thing

There is no way to be known for what you do if you do *everything*. There is no way to be known for what you do if you help *everybody*. You're going to pick. I can't tell you how many people have said to me, "But Dr. Una, I can't pick just one thing!"

Yes you can. And you have to.

If you decide to help everybody and do all the things in all kinds of ways, it's going to be very diffuse, and you're going to throw away so much energy and you're not going to make it to the other side.

I get that you have a lot of passions and want to do a lot of things. I do too. And I'll let you in on an exciting secret. Once you establish your first business and become well-known for that one thing you do, you can start another business and another. I own three businesses and a non-profit and I'm not stopping there.

But first you have to focus on *one* thing. You're going to own *one* thing. You're going to pick up that hammer and keep hitting the wall in *one* spot over and over again until you break through to the other side.

Because guess what happens when you get to the other side? You can do *all the things*. Look at Beyoncé. Beyoncé is an artist. She started out years ago as an artist, just singing and dancing. That's all she was doing, and she was hitting at that. Then she becomes the Beyoncé that everybody in the whole world knows. She breaks through. She's known. Very well-known. Now she can have a skincare line, a movie production company, and a clothing line. She can do anything and everything she wants to do because she has broken through to the other side.

Before you break through to the other side, your only job is to break through to that other side. You need focus. Focus, focus, focus. This requires a lot of discipline, but when you get this right, everything else works. When this isn't right, nothing else works.

So you focus on one thing. In order to focus on one thing, you're going to need three healthy obsessions.

Three Healthy Obsessions You Absolutely Need

You're going to need to be obsessed (in a good way) about three things: who you help; what pain they have; and what outcome you offer them.

Healthy obsession #1: Who do I help?

Who is my ideal client? "Everybody" is never the answer. You'll never break through the wall that way. You're going to pick a person. Who do you help?

As for me, I help physicians. Specifically, physicians who want to build profitable 6-, 7- and multiple-7-figure businesses. Each of the doctors I work with also helps a specific kind of person. If you go to my social media profile, you'll see that I'm really active. But I only talk to one person: the physician who wants to build profitable businesses. That's who I talk to. I don't talk to anyone else, not on social media. I use that for my business.

Who do you help? You want to know this person inside and out. You want to be clear on who this person is. And you want to be focused on serving that person in the way only you can.

Ask yourself: who do I help?

Healthy obsession #2: What pain do they have?

The more you can understand the pain of the person you help, the more people will raise their hands and say, "Oh my goodness, she gets me. I want to work with her."

What is the pain that they have? What keeps them up at night? If your ideal client were to wake up in the middle of the night and break out into a sweat, what are they thinking? When they show up in groups, what are they talking about? What makes them cry? What is their pain?

The more you know that—and the better you can articulate it in words that resonate with them—the more people will flock to you. I know this sounds simple, but it's so profound. This is how we become known for what we do.

Let me use EntreMD as an example. I already told you who I help—physicians who want to build profitable businesses so they can live life and practice medicine on their terms. What pain do they have? They have the fear of failure. They don't have a business education. They have the fear of putting themselves out there. There's a fear of selling (physicians aren't supposed to sell things). There's a fear of leading a team (they haven't done that before). There's the fear of coming up with enough content. There's a fear of being able to afford to pay another physician in their practice (a multiple six-figure investment). It's all of these things.

I'm in tune with their pain points. That's where all my podcast episodes come from. That's where this book is coming from. The people I help and the pain they're feeling. I know their pain, and I know it well.

Ask yourself: what pain does my client have?

Healthy obsession #3: What outcome do I offer them?

What could their life look like if they decide to work with me? What does life look like on the other side of working with me?

I help physicians who want to build profitable businesses. I just listed many of their fears. What is the outcome I'm offering them? Visibility. What could their lives look like once their business is visible, once they become known for what they do? I paint that picture for them.

Life could look like: I have revenue confidence, and I know how to build a 6-, 7-, multiple 7-figure business. It could look like: I now have financial freedom. It could look like: I paid off $260k in school loans. It could look like: I built a team and, because of that, I'm able to take twice as much time off every year. There are so many things it could look like. I'm in tune with that, and I know how to communicate it clearly to them.

Ask yourself: what outcome do I offer them?

How do you know if your message is a good one? Well, the only foolproof way is to get it out in the world, amplify it, and see how people respond.

The more you understand who you help, the pain they have, and the outcome you can offer them, the more people will follow you, follow your brand, choose to work with you, call you to speak on stages, refer to you, and all of that.

If you understand these three things, if you focus on these three healthy obsessions until you break through Sheehan's Wall, then you can do anything your heart desires. Because you're known for what you do.

You Don't Outgrow the Basics

You might be thinking, "Dr. Una, I've learned this already." That's great. Are you still working on it? Are you applying it? Are you implementing it consistently?"

Let me tell you something. I am a student of business. I have studied this. This is my hobby. I study successful 7-, 8-, and 9-figure businesses to see what they're doing. At *this* stage, what is working? At *that* stage, what is working?

Let me tell you what every last one of these successful businesses is doing: they're fine-tuning their ideal client, the pain they have, and the outcome they're offering them. And they're figuring out the best ways to articulate that.

Somebody who is building a 9-figure business is still working on this. So what do you think we should be working on? Should we be working on this too? It's a no-brainer.

You don't outgrow the basics. That's like LeBron James saying "I've outgrown the two-point shot." No way. He works on his shot every single day. You don't outgrow the basics; you just get better at them. You don't outgrow the basics; you master them.

I want to make sure that you get this. I don't want you to just memorize it and say these are the three healthy obsessions I need to have. I want you to be able to apply this. I want you to be able to tweak your business. The truth of the matter is this: I want this book to be the book that changes everything for your business. Whether ultimately you're someone who ever works with us or not. I want this book to be that gamechanger for you.

But it's up to you and you alone.

Five Things That Might Get In Your Way

So let's talk about five things that might get in your way (and let's get them *out* of your way right now). We've alluded to some of these, but I want to spell them out very clearly, because you've got to get past these limiting mindsets if you want your business to thrive.

#1: I want to help everybody.

There are eight billion people on this planet. Can you really help everybody? Of course you can't. So, when that thought comes to you, I want you to remind yourself that it's not only impossible, but it can sabotage your ability to help the very people you're actually uniquely equipped to help. You don't want that.

When you meet someone and they ask what you do, and you say, "I help *these* people and I do *this* thing and I do *that* thing and I help *these* people over here." Wait a minute, what? That's so confusing. It's not focused. We don't know what you *actually* do.

A confused mind never buys.

This is something I learned years ago and I've never forgotten. A confused mind never buys. We cannot communicate confusion. We have to make things crystal clear. We've got to make sure our ideal client knows who we help: them. Even the best idea is worthless if you can't communicate it effectively to your ideal client. The clearer we are, the more we can explode our businesses in the best possible way.

"I want to help everybody" is a myth. It's a lie. When you think about it, you simply cannot help everybody. So give that up.

#2: I can't choose.

That's not true. You can choose. You've made hard choices before. You're a physician. There's evidence that you can choose. There are so many medical schools. You chose one. There are so many fields of medicine. You chose one. There are so many residencies you could have done. You chose one.

If you're married, you chose somebody. If you own a car, you chose one. So don't believe the lie. There's evidence to the contrary. You can choose.

Say to yourself: I'm going to choose. I'm going to choose who I work with. I'm going to choose who my business is going to serve. I am going to choose.

We're going to choose. This is the person I want to serve. This is the problem I want to solve. This is the outcome I want to give them. We're going to choose.

#3: Too many people already do what I do.

Have you had this thought? It's a common one. But let's backtrack and look at facts. There is a physician shortage in the United States, and the projection is that it's about to get a whole lot worse. There are a million physicians, and somehow there's still a shortage. As long as there are still people out there with the problem you solve, there are not enough people doing what you do.

Why did I start the EntreMD Business School when there's Harvard Business School and hundreds of other business schools? Because it's needed. Because it serves a specific population. Because physicians don't get a business education in med school. Because there are so many physicians out there who need what I have to offer.

Stop thinking (and saying) that there are too many people doing what you do. Start saying that there aren't *enough* people doing what you do.

#4: I know the pain and desires of my ideal client.

That right there can cost you millions of dollars. Do not get overconfident and assume that you know your client's pain and desires. You don't. You don't know their desires. It's like a doctor saying they don't need a patient to tell them what to write in the History of Presenting Illness (HPI) because they know exactly what the person is thinking. We would never say, "I know exactly what their pain is, and I'm going to make up the HPI myself."

We don't know until we ask them. We don't know until we observe. We don't know. So we take the time to listen to them. And they tell us their pain and desires. This is so important.

Maybe you already have a wildly successful business and you're sitting there thinking, I'm going to introduce this new vertical into my business. This is going to be great. This is going to help my patients because this is what they need.

I'm here to tell you that people don't pay for what they *need*. They pay for what they *want*. You don't know what they want unless you ask them—and listen carefully to what they say.

When you get a great idea, the smartest thing you can do is go to the market and listen to your people and see if there's any resonance. See if that's what they want. See if that's what they care about. There's a big gap between what people *need* and what people *want*. Talk to your people. Find out what they actually want deep down inside.

When we started building the EntreMD Business School, I could have built out a curriculum and told my students: this is what you should know. But, instead, what we've done over the years is this: we lay the basic foundation and then we listen.

- Where are they getting stuck?
- What do they need/want?
- What is keeping them up at night?
- What are the limiting beliefs that are getting in their way?
- What is the outcome they're looking for?

Then we build something to solve that problem.

Your business is not about you. Your business is about who you serve. When you go to where your ideal clients are—like when they're in a Facebook group and they're talking—you're paying attention. What are they complaining about? What are their pain points? What do they wish for? The more you understand that—and the better you can say it in their language—the more you resonate with them, the more they're like, "Oh my goodness, she gets me. This is the doctor for me, the coach for me, the product for me."

The more you know what they want, the more you resonate with them, the more they say yes, the more you become a category of one. The more you become a thought leader. It's all tied to you being able to get inside the head of your ideal client. Asking good questions and listening well are such critical skills. This right here will put you in a position to serve a lot of people and earn a lot of money. Serve and earn.

There are a number of people who, whenever I post on social media, say things like, "There you are again! You're in my head!" Yes, that is my full-time job—to be in your head. And I take my job very seriously.

This is where most of my podcast episodes come from. I don't make up stuff off the top of my head. I get inside of my ideal clients' heads. I listen to their questions and concerns and turn it into a podcast episode. I'm responding to their pain, their needs and wants, and that's why my podcast resonates so deeply with them.

I know the pain and desires of my ideal clients.

#5: I've got this. I don't need any help.

This one is for all the veteran entrepreneurs out there—or for any entrepreneur who thinks they have nothing to learn. When I hear people say, "I don't need this. I've got this," I'm so scared for them. Oh my goodness, stop saying "I've got this." I have been in rooms with some of the most phenomenal entrepreneurs. I could drop all kinds of names. They're doing $100 million in revenue, $500 million in revenue.

Let me tell you something about each of these successful people. They almost always have a beginner's mindset. They're curious. You'll see someone running a $130 million company listening to someone who just launched and is celebrating their first $100k. They're just listening, like, "Huh, how did you do that? What were you thinking when you did that? Talk to me about that strategy."

This right here is why they are running such a phenomenally successful business. They stay humble and curious and they never, ever stop learning. Please do yourself a huge favor and refuse to say, "I've got this. I don't need to learn any more. That's too basic, too foundational."

We never outgrow our foundation, friends. How many floors does a building need to be for it to no longer need a foundation? Think about it. "I'm a whole high-rise building in downtown Atlanta. I don't need a foundation." Never! Never. You never outgrow the foundation; you never outgrow the basics. You become a master by mastering the basics. Please don't say I've got this. Stay hungry, stay humble, stay learning.

That also means that, the longer you're an entrepreneur, the easier it is for you to get out of touch.

You're no longer able to resonate with your ideal client, because you're no longer attentive to them. You're no longer listening to them. You don't know what their pain points are. It's been a long long time since you were in their shoes, and you've forgotten what it feels like.

Not to mention that the world is changing faster than we ever imagined it could. In the past four years, we had a whole pandemic, then hyper-inflation and a recession, then the Great Resignation. You best believe that their pain is evolving. There are new pains coming up in the realm of what you do for them. You have to stay humble and curious, so you can find out what that is, so you can evolve what you're doing so you can be relevant now. Otherwise you expire. And they find someone else who's actually in touch with what they want.

"I got this already" is a pitfall. Don't do it. *Don't do it.*

Business vs. Charity

At the end of this chapter, you'll find a link to a workbook. I want you to print it out and work through it. It's going to require making some big decisions like identifying your ideal client. Before you make that big decision, I need to make something very clear, something that trips up a lot of physicians.

Here's the deal. As doctors, we love people. We just do. And very often, we're okay with building businesses that aren't profitable, as long as we can help people. In fact, you might be thinking, "Dr. Una, I really want to serve the underserved, the underrepresented, the people who do not have the access to what I do."

I hear you. And you can absolutely do that. But that is a charity, not a business. Those are two very different models. A business is a business, and a charity is a charity. You keep the business things in the business and the charity things in the charity. If you run a business, and all the people you're serving in your business are people who cannot pay you, your business will close its doors.

You want to be a philanthropist? I feel you. I'm a philanthropist too. And this is how you make philanthropy work. In your business, you make all the cash you can. Then you build a charity and funnel as much cash as you want to it. But charity principles don't work in a business. They operate very differently, and you need to keep them as separate entities.

A business is an entity that serves people and creates a profit. If you do not have a profit, you will have to fire your staff, give up your building, and shut your doors. As a responsible entrepreneur with a charitable heart, you will serve a lot and earn a lot—so you can give a lot.

If you don't care about money and just want to serve humanity, that's fine. But you need money to serve humanity. So make that money in your business, then take everything from your business and put it into your charity and serve people who can't pay you. On the charity side, that will work. You can't just primarily serve the underserved in your business. Entrepreneurship is an economic game, a money game. You serve and you earn. You *have* to earn.

The beautiful thing about physicians is that we don't put profit before people. This is why we make such wonderful entrepreneurs. We're here to serve people. But you have to serve *and* earn. They're right there together. They go hand in hand.

After you earn the money, then by all means, give it all away. But the only way to run a business—and to *keep* your business—is to make it profitable. So one of the best things you can do if you truly love humanity and you want to serve humanity, is learn to create profitable businesses. And then you give it all away.

We're making big decisions here. And I don't want you making charity decisions in a business. Own both of them. But put the rules where they belong.

Your Workbook: Simple but Serious

In just a moment, you're going to finish reading this chapter, print out the workbook, and start filling it out. It's a simple workbook. Everything I do is simple. I don't like complicated things. But it will require some brainpower, and you will need to make some big decisions. We're doing the heavy lifting right now so we can have fun throughout the rest of the book.

One of the biggest decisions you will make is: **who is my ideal client?** Your ideal client is somebody who has a problem you solve. They are aware that they have the problem. They are looking for a solution. And they are willing and able to pay.

Each one of these pieces is crucial, so I'm going to repeat them. Your ideal client has a problem you solve. They're aware of the problem. They're actively seeking a solution to this problem. They're willing to pay, and they're able to pay.

You're going to fill that out in the workbook and own it.

Then you're going to write down the pain they have, the problem you can solve for them. Now, remember, their pain isn't always what you think. You may think they have a chronic disease and that's their pain. And they may be thinking, "I just want to lose weight." Or "I don't want to lose my foot like Uncle Jones." When they come to you, what are they complaining about? What are they saying they want you to help them with? Use their words, not yours. And to use their words, you've got to be actively listening to them.

Then you're going to write down the outcome you're offering them. The pain, then the outcome. What can life look like after they're done working with you? Paint that picture.

Let me give you an example from my own business. My ideal clients are physicians who are committed to building 6-, 7- and multiple 7-figure companies so they can live life and practice medicine on their terms.

Here's what I would say to my ideal client: Hey, you're a physician. I know people have told you that physicians can't thrive as entrepreneurs—and they definitely can't build 7-figure businesses. I know they want you to believe that private practice is dead and all of that. But let me tell you why I'm here and what I can help you do. Dr. X joined the EntreMD Business School, built a dominant brand and a team, took their practice to multiple 7-figures, and has more time off now than they've ever had. Private equity came to them with an offer to buy them out, and this doc said like a boss, "That's not a good deal. I could do better by myself." And so they did. And you can do this too.

You're Building the Foundation

Once you've nailed down your business idea, decided on your ideal client, and identified their pain/problem and the outcome you can offer them, you've built the foundation of your business. I know you're itching to get to the Visibility Formula, where you put yourself out there in front of everyone so people can get to know, like, and trust you—and ultimately decide to work with you—but the foundation comes first.

Remember—you're making big decisions, big choices, right now. You're not going with all seven of your great business ideas (not until you're Beyoncé anyway). You're choosing *one*. We're going to have these babies one at a time. You can choose, and you can choose right. You're going to choose that one big idea and focus on that until you break through that wall to the other side where you become known for what you do.

This chapter was all about putting on our coveralls and building the foundation. Once we've got our message, we can answer the question: how do I amplify this? How do I put this everywhere? How do I get people to say to me, "Oh my goodness, you're everywhere. Everywhere I look, there's your brand."

If there's anybody who should be everywhere, it's physicians.

And I'm going to help you get there. The next chapter is all about developing omnipresence with our brands. Are you ready? Head over to <u>www.entremd.com/visiblitybook</u> to download your workbook, fill it out, then it's on to Chapter 2.

EBS Student Spotlight: Dr. Emeka Obidi

Dr. Emeka Obidi is a pediatrician and the CEO of Partners in Pediatrics and Family Health, a family practice in Western Maryland. He's also the CEO of Newborn Prep Academy, where he helps new (and expectant) moms learn how to care for their newborns confidently. He helps them release mom guilt and truly enjoy their babies.

Dr. Obidi joined EBS in 2022. Prior to that, he was a physician entrepreneur who had been "recently bitten by the entrepreneurial bug." He had done a little bit of coaching, but he lacked the confidence he needed to be truly successful.

He has worked at his practice for 17+ years. The first eight years he felt like he was just trying to keep his head above water. He's owned the practice for the last nine years, and he has been successful. It was multi-seven figure practice; he was able to make payroll; and he knew they would be able to get through the pandemic without firing anyone or slashing hours. And they still made more money that year, but he was plagued with self-doubt, a lot of imposter syndrome. "I just felt like I didn't know what I was doing," he says.

He had listened to the EntreMD podcast and found great value in it, so he decided to attend my Visibility Formula workshop. He said that my homework assignments blew his mind. Prior to that, he'd done maybe one or two Facebook lives and a couple videos to promote his online business, but he hadn't done them confidently. I told him to get out there, introduce himself on his platform, and tell people what his business is all about, so he did it. And he was blown away by the engagement from his audience.

"I was surprised at how simple it was," he says, "to just go on there and say, 'Hi, I'm Dr. Obidi. This is what I do. Thank you for being part of practice.'" He talked about his practice and his passion for his patients. And his audience responded in a big way.

There was a podcast he wanted to be on, but he figured he'd wait a year or so until his business had grown a little bigger, a little better. Then he decided to just go for it, and the host said yes.

"I was so taken aback by the success from taking those small simple steps," he says. "If I could benefit this much from a few days in a free workshop, I knew there had to be a whole lot more in the business school—which has not failed to deliver. It's been an amazing ride so far."

When he joined EBS, we had a one-on-one session, and I gave him some advice about the structure and focus of his business that he says set him on a different path he wouldn't have found on his own. "Instead of distractions," he says, "I'm now focused on my business and it's really grown revenue-wise."

He says the visibility has been incredible. He's grown more confident in front of the camera and can speak off the cuff now without having to have all his notes super prepared. For the first assignment where I told them to introduce themselves to their audience, he waited until everyone had left the building and it was completely quiet. Now he just puts a sticker on his door that says "live recording in progress—don't bother me." He was on Facebook Live a few months ago, and his kids were in the room making faces at him, and he asked them to come on camera and say hi to the audience. That's something he never would have done at the beginning.

"It's going to be uncomfortable initially," he tells people who are just getting started, "but embrace it, because it does get better. You do get more comfortable."

He credits the teaching in EBS and the discipline to show up on camera week after week after week. "We've had patients come to the practice just because of seeing my content online," he says, "which would not happen if I hadn't attended the Visibility Formula workshop and been part of the business school. It's been really an amazing experience on a personal level."

Another amazing experience has been his ability to rearrange his schedule and get home earlier to spend more time with his family—while still seeing the same number of patients. He didn't have the capacity or the mindset to do that before joining EBS. "Because of the container I'm in right now," he says, "I'm able to look at my calendar or the situation and say, 'Okay, instead of saying this is not possible, I'm asking how can this be possible?'"

His next goal is to take more vacation time in the coming year while still making more money than he did last year. In the past, he just assumed he'd have to work more to make more, but he's had a paradigm shift in his thinking. He's renegotiating his contracts with the insurance companies.

"I'm going to get so much more money for the same things I'm already doing," he says. "Because of my EBS training, I was able to show up to the negotiation table with more confidence. Thanks to EBS, I appreciate what I bring to the table as a physician entrepreneur. I know I was a good physician, but I bought the lie that I'm *just* a physician and not a good business person. But that's bullcrap. For the first time, I understand how my training as a physician really prepared me to be a fantastic entrepreneur."

He knew that his physician training prepared him to work hard, but he never realized how transferable all his skills were in the business world as well. All he was thinking about was the fact that he had no experience in entrepreneurship. Then EBS helped him see that he wasn't experienced with seeing patients at the beginning either. Once he gained experience, there were so many things he could do with his eyes closed.

Physicians have tenacity and the ability to do hard things with courage. "I know a lot of people are afraid of business," he says, "but it's only because they haven't set their minds to it. We were all afraid in med school, initially, but we had all set our minds to be in med school and, even though we were afraid, we still showed up and did the work. And it's the same thing in business. You're able to just step on the stage and just do what needs to be done, regardless of how you feel. That's probably one of the greatest things I've benefited from being part of this amazing community."

CHAPTER 2:

How to Amplify Your Message to Attract All the Clients You Want

An omnipresent business and brand is the dream, right? Imagine being in front of all your ideal clients, in front of all your referral sources, in front of all the people who can get you speaking gigs, in front of all the podcasts you'd love to be a guest on. Imagine people saying, "Oh my gosh, you're everywhere." Wouldn't you love that??

Guess what. I'm here to tell you that it's possible. It's possible to build a brand where you're everywhere. It's possible to build a brand that is so focused you can crash through Sheehan's Wall.

It is possible to set your business up in such a way that, when people think of the problem you solve, your name is top of mind. Out of everyone else in the world, they think of you *first*. That's huge.

When we say "the happiest place on earth," people think of Disney. When we say "car insurance," people think of Geico or State Farm or Progressive. What if, for the thing you do, your name comes up for people?

To get to that place, we can't stay in our current reality. We have to reject the status quo. We have to choose to uplevel. We have to own this. When people think of the problem I solve and the solution I offer, my name is what comes up. MY NAME. Own that picture.

And don't forget—fear will show up. It always does. But we're not going to let it stop us. If you're terrified, you're in great company. I've done everything I've done scared. It's good. You're fine. We're going to work through this together, and it's going to be amazing.

We're Not Learning to Know; We're Learning to Do

The Visibility Formula is not about reading a few thousand words and acquiring new knowledge. It's about moving forward. It's about learning how to amplify your message and then getting out there and actually doing what you learned.

When I do the Visibility Formula workshop and people get out there and do their homework on that first night, they gain huge traction right from the very beginning. This is how you create snowballs in your business. This is how you create bigger wins. This is how you put yourself out there and become an opportunity magnet.

You do the work.

If you did your homework from Chapter 1, you've built your foundation. You're clear on your message. You know who your ideal client is, what their problem is, and what their life can look like after they work with you.

And now we're going to put our businesses and brands on blast.

Let's Make Our Business Omnipresent

I've said this over and over again (and I'll keep saying it): don't read a book or attend a workshop or pay for coaching from someone who hasn't *actually done the thing* you want to do. You want to amplify your message and get your business out in front of people and experience growth? I can show you how to do that, because I've done it. I have the receipts.

EntreMD just hit #315 on the Inc. 5000 List for fastest-growing privately held companies in the United States. When they measured our growth over a three-year period, it was 1816%. That's wild. And the principles we used to get that exponential growth are the same ones I'll be talking about in this book. I'm not about fluff (just ask the students in the EntreMD Business School). I'm going to get down to business in this book. This is the real deal.

And please don't be tempted to think, "But yeah, you're Dr. Una. I'm not as good at business as you. You're a natural." Listen carefully. This is not a Dr. Una thing. This can work for everyone. Let me give you some examples.

One doctor, an EBS student, launched a direct specialty care practice that was profitable from day one. She really wanted to pay off her school loans of $260k and boom, she did it. Another doctor made $2k in coaching before joining EBS. A year after joining, she made $138k. I have testimonial after testimonial I could share (and I'll be sharing some throughout the book).

These principles work.

So how do we put our brand everywhere? Before we get into the tactics, we need to make sure we come to a place where we're absolutely committed to the results we want. I want you to believe in yourself and know that this will work for your business.

Even if you don't have a business yet, *you have a business.* Your business is called "Dr. You, Incorporated." Your personal brand is your business, and all the things you'll learn here are things you can apply to your personal brand. Then, if you decide you want to go and do something else, you already have all the skills you need to make that work.

In the EntreMD Business School, we call that *the business before the business.* We don't wait. We start. We take immediate action and figure it out as we go.

When I teach the Visibility Formula in a workshop format, I take a poll and ask these questions:

- What's your primary business?

- What's your revenue goal?
- On a scale of 1-5, how committed are you to this goal?
- How many patients/clients do you need to hit the goal?
- What platform (not your own) would you like to show up on weekly?

I'll go ahead and ask you to answer these questions too. Now, answers will vary of course, but I'll tell you that, for the commitment question, I want the same answer for everyone. I want you to be all the way committed — a 5 on the commitment scale. This level of commitment makes me super excited because, when people are truly committed, they achieve what they set out to do.

Now let's talk about your clients.

All the Clients You Will Ever Need Already Exist

I want you to read this next sentence very carefully. *All the clients you will ever need already exist.* If we understand that, then when it comes to marketing, we're just showing up enough so they can find us.

They already exist.

It's not like there are no patients or clients. Of course there are. We are no longer going to make the statement "there are no clients," because that is lower level thinking. We're going to ask a great question: *how can I put myself in front of my client?* Because they already exist. All the clients you will ever need already exist.

The second thing is this: *they're already gathered somewhere.* Your ideal clients are all gathered somewhere because of what they share in common—this problem or pain point or question they have that you have the solution for. Humans are social beings. They already exist and someone has done an amazing job of gathering them. They're not with you, but they exist, and they're gathered somewhere.

You just need to go where they're gathered.

Their attention has already been grabbed by somebody. Somebody came along before you and did the work of congregating them in one central location. So your job is to show up where they are and let them know about you and your business.

In this chapter, we won't be talking about showing up on social media. We won't be talking about starting your own podcast or YouTube channel. That's coming. First we're going to talk about going where your clients are. All the clients you need already exist and they are somewhere, which means you can hit your revenue goals for this year if you find out where that place is and get your message in front of them.

Remember who your ideal client is. Your ideal client has a problem. They're aware that they have the problem. They want the solution. They're willing and able to pay. These people are actively looking for you. They're gathered somewhere. They just don't know about you.

But they're about to find out.

Where Are Your Clients Gathered?

Let's talk about some of the places where your clients are already gathered. None of this will be rocket science, but we don't need rocket science. We just need to grab a proven strategy—that has worked for thousands of successful entrepreneurs—and run with it.

So where are your clients hanging out? Well, a good number of your clients listen to podcasts. If somebody is trying to reach physician entrepreneurs, where are they? They listen to the EntreMD podcast. If that person were to come and be a guest on my podcast, guess what. They just got access to thousands of physicians who are entrepreneurs. They're casting a pretty wide net.

Can you see how just *one guest appearance* on a podcast leads to amazing visibility in front of a whole bunch of your ideal clients? Before they came on my show, there were thousands of people who didn't know them. Then they showed up on my podcast where I've worked hard to gather thousands of physicians who listen and subscribe, and now those thousands of people know this person. Can we just take a moment and appreciate how magical that is?

Guest spots on other people's platforms are the granddaddy of promoting your content. You're accessing their entire audience and, on top of that, the host is lending you his or her credibility. My podcast audience already knows, likes, and trusts me. If I have someone on my podcast, that gives that person credibility with my audience that they wouldn't have had otherwise.

Is this a lightbulb moment for you? It's super simple, but so often, people just aren't thinking like this. They think they need to go out and find their ideal clients one by one. They think they have to find a magic way to get their ideal clients to come to them.

No, you just have to go where they're already gathered.

Your ideal client listens to podcasts. They read blogs. They watch YouTube videos. We have a doctor who is an alumnus of EntreMD Business School, and she has a YouTube channel where she teaches people how to write research papers. If somebody is trying to get to doctors who do research, they need to go be a guest on her YouTube channel, because she has already gathered their ideal clients.

If you're a pediatrician and there's a local OB-GYN with a YouTube channel that all these moms follow, and you go on that channel as a guest, you've now put yourself in front of hundreds, even thousands of potential clients. That host lent you their credibility and now all those moms know you're the pediatrician to go to once their babies are born.

In addition to podcasts, blogs, and YouTube channels, your ideal clients go to events like Open Houses, networking events, local groups, retreats, industry conferences and online events on social media. A bunch of your ideal clients are already gathered in these spaces. If you will do the work of going to where they're all gathered, you will amplify your message in ways you can't do from your own social media platform.

Once you have your message, it's like a candle. Your job is to light it and put it on a stand. You have your message, and now you're going to put it in these groups, so you can amplify it, so people can find you.

We think (and hope) that once we have a great product or service, people will just find it, love it, buy it. But it doesn't work that way. If you don't tell people about it, your service will be the world's best-kept secret. That's the last thing we want it to be.

We don't want to be a secret. We want to be a household name. We want to be in a category of one. We want to be synonymous with the problem we solve. When someone has that problem, we want our name to keep popping up. We want to be known—very well known—for what we do.

Yes, going to where your ideal clients are gathered and putting yourself out there might be a little scary—especially if you're an introvert. But you can choose to commit to it anyway, and do it. I did it, and it changed my business and my life.

Do What the Big Dogs Are Doing

Like I've said, I'm a student of business. I carefully study people who are running successful 7-, 8-, and 9-figure businesses so I can do what they do. When I say study, I mean *study*. One of the things that baffles me (but that I really love) is that what we're talking about now might seem simple, but these successful business owners are doing the exact same thing.

I was just talking to somebody who did $43 million in revenue last year and she told me she shows up as a guest on four podcasts a month. Every single month. If someone who's making $43 million is doing that, what do you think we should do? Do you think we should maybe do that too? Yeah, I think so too. Let's do that. Let's do what that 8-figure business owner is doing.

Two years ago, I spoke to Kara Goldin, the founder of Hint, Inc., which is known for their unsweetened flavored Hint water. The previous year, her business did $150 million in revenue. She wrote and launched a book called *Undaunted* in 2020. Now I'm pretty sure that someone who launched a book and is making $150 million in annual revenue could just do some paid advertising, and her book would sell. But she did 240 guest interviews over a three-month period to get the word out about her book.

The third person I was blown away by was John Lee Dumas. He's the host of a podcast called *Entrepreneurs on Fire*. This man is the definition of hardcore. He gets over a million downloads a month. If the EntreMD

Podcast had a million downloads a month, I could launch a book and just mention it at the beginning of my podcast episodes. And I wouldn't try to market, because I wouldn't need to do it, right?

Is that what John Lee Dumas did? Did he sit back and just mention his book on his own podcast? Of course not. He did 300 guest interviews in 2 months. Unsurprisingly, his book became a best seller of best sellers and brought in an unbelievable amount of revenue—not just from the book but also business he got from that.

I'll share one more example, and this one really shocked me. When Michelle Obama wrote her memoir, *Becoming,* I was so curious to see her launch strategy. She's the former First Lady. Everybody knows her, right? Like literally everybody in the whole country knows her—and most of the people around the rest of the world as well. Michelle Obama should just be able to say, "Guys, I wrote a book!" and everybody buys the book, right? And it's a bestseller, the end.

Instead, this woman went on to do a 32-city tour in 6 months. In every city she went to, there was something before the main event, the main event, then some social thing she did afterward. Three whole days for every single city. Think about the number of flights, the number of hotel rooms, the number of times she had to get her hair and make-up done, the number of people she had to talk to and shake hands with and take selfies with. Think of all that goes into a tour this elaborate.

But that's why her book is on track to be the best-selling memoir *of all time.*

For all these heavy hitters, when they want to amplify their message, they go outside of their brand. Cara Goldin and John Lee Dumas were guests on hundreds of podcasts, and Michelle Obama toured the entire country.

They're putting themselves out there and getting in front of people who will buy their books. We're going to do that too. It might be on a smaller scale (at least at first), but we're going to do what the ultra successful do.

Embrace the Fear

Sometimes people will tell me, "I'm posting on social media and nothing's working." And I ask them: *what is supporting your social media?* You can't just post on social media. The thing that supports your social media is the thing you do to put yourself out there so that the people who don't know you can find you.

If you're not putting yourself out there, and you're just posting to your own social media, no new people are going to find you.

Now, if you haven't noticed, we haven't even talked about social media or your own podcast yet. We'll talk about that in the next chapter. This chapter is all about: what am I going to do to put myself all the way out there so people who don't know me can find me?

Some of you are scared reading this, thinking, "But I don't *want* to be out there. I don't want to be a guest on other people's podcasts. I don't want to do an Instagram live with someone. I'm afraid."

Let me remind you of what we talked about in the last chapter. I asked you about your commitment, regardless of the fear you're feeling. You were warned. You were warned about fear. The fear is inevitable. It comes with the territory. It will always and forever be present when you're about to step outside your comfort zone.

But we don't let fear stop us. We do it anyway. We do it scared. We all feel fear, so we're in good company. We're all feeling the fear and we're all going to *do it anyway.*

Let me tell you something that has helped me so much as an entrepreneur. I've said it before, but the best things bear repeating. Are you ready?

My business is not about me.

If that seems weird to you, I get it. You might be thinking, wait a minute. It's *my* business. Of course it's about me.

Hear me out. My business does not exist for me. If that were the case, I'd go out of business really quickly, because I wouldn't have any clients. My business exists to serve someone. That person has a pain; they have a problem. That problem keeps them up at night. That problem, for some people, has taken years away from their lives. That problem is keeping them from becoming the best version of themselves. That problem is putting them into a position where they've gone five years with a dream that has not become a reality. It has affected their health, their relationships and their finances.

That person is actively looking for me, hoping that today is the day that I show up in their lives. They need to find me, so I can help them solve their problem and live their best life. They need me to show up.

So what do I do? I show up for that person. I may be nervous. I may be scared. I may think it's a little messy—I don't have this perfected yet. It doesn't matter. My business doesn't exist for me. The more I forget about myself, the more I leave myself out of the equation, the better entrepreneur I become.

My business does not exist for me.

Repeat that to yourself over and over again. Write it on a sticky note and put it on your bathroom mirror. My business is not about me. My business is about somebody else who has a problem I can solve. I have the experience and the knowledge and the skill set to solve their exact problem, and they're willing and able to pay me to solve that problem for them. They win. I win. We all win.

That's what it's about. If you remember this, it will serve you very well.

Why am I here today writing this book? It's not about me. It's about every one of you reading this book. Thirty days from now, I want people sliding into my DMs saying, "Dr. Una, you won't believe what happened after I did what you wrote about in your book!"

Of course I'll believe it. Tell me.

"Dr. Una, I've been trying to do this for two years. Then I read your book, and I did it! You will not believe this!"

Oh yes I will. Tell me all about it. I love celebrating with you. All day every day. Tell me all about it.

So you're going to embrace your fears, put yourself out there, and it's going to work. Putting yourself out there works. It works better than just about any other thing you will ever do. We just have to be committed — and dare our fears.

Tips for Putting Yourself Out There

I'm going to go ahead and tell you what your homework will be at the end of this chapter. It's exciting, maybe a little intimidating. It's also nothing very earth-shattering, but if you do this, it will change your life and your business forever. It really will.

You're going to get yourself out there on three different people's platforms — their podcast, their YouTube channel, their IG live, their virtual or in-person event.

Before you say, "That's impossible. I can't do that!" I want you to read to the end of the chapter, because you can absolutely do this.

Let me introduce you to someone who embraced this challenge during a Visibility Formula workshop earlier this year, and look what happened.

Dr. Carolina Sueldo says she signed up for the Visibility Formula workshop on a whim. She's a double-board-certified OB-GYN and fertility specialist with a move from California to Florida on horizon.

"I knew I wanted more," she says. "I knew there were changes coming."

She remembers me saying, "Treat this like a paid event. Put your whole self into it and do the best you can." She decided that was exactly what she was going to do, and she did.

During the workshop, she connected with several people on different points in their journey and by the end of the week, she had booked four podcast episodes and three Instagram lives. Then, a month or so after the event, she hosted a virtual postpartum perinatal women's health summit with other experts and had a huge turnout. "It really catapulted my brand," she says.

At the time, she didn't realize just how big it would all turn out to be. Her summit coincided with National Infertility Awareness Week. She had booked local TV interviews and become somewhat of a go-to person after they aired. They had been looking for someone, and they found her. Because of those local connections, she landed a CNN interview shortly after Roe v. Wade was overturned. "It really was this spiral that kind of took on a life of its own," she says.

Since then, she's been a regular guest on podcasts. "And the jumping off point for all of it was the Visibility Formula," she told me.

Did you catch what she said? People were looking for someone to speak on infertility but they didn't have access to someone. People are looking for you, but they have no idea where to find you. They don't have access to you. *Give them access to you.* Once you start showing up, you become a magnet for opportunities.

It's so worth facing—and embracing— the fear of putting yourself out there. So incredibly worth it.

Where Do I Find My Ideal Client?

Not long ago I did a one-on-one VIP day with a client who told me she didn't know how to find her ideal clients. "I don't know where these people are," she said.

So I pulled up this really complicated software that can help you find things. I typed in "women professional event [name of city]" and boom. There were all the clients. Remember—all the clients you'll ever need already exist. And they're gathered somewhere. And there's a really complex software you can use that will help you find them instantly.

It's called Google.

If you want to find your ideal client, simply find out what podcasts they listen to, what blogs they're reading, what events they're attending. Be disciplined. Do the work.

How do we find this information? Well, first of all, we can ask them. All the people you ever need to know are connected to people you know now. Ask those people you do know, and it broadens your circle.

You can also use this hack. (it's top secret, so don't tell anyone) Go to Google and type in "[name of your competitor]" and "podcasts" and you'll see all the places where they've been a podcast guest. Now go confidently pitch yourself to each and every one of those podcasts. Tell them why their audience needs to hear from you.

Then do it again with your competitor's name + "YouTube" and again with their name + "blogs" and you'll get a big inventory of all the places they've been. Chances are, those YouTube channels and blogs are the right audience for you too.

I love this hack because it works. And it saves more time and energy than you can imagine.

One physician told me, "I don't see any pediatricians doing podcasts." I told them to be the first. And remember, you're not looking for where the *pediatricians* are. You're looking for where the *moms* are gathered. What podcasts are these moms listening to? They might be listening to some just for fun, and they're probably listening to some that help solve a particular parenting problem they have. Do your research, figure out where those moms are gathered, and be a guest on those podcasts.

Your homework at the end of this chapter might be a little scary, but do it, and it will literally change your business and your life. You're going to get three guest spots on other people's podcasts, YouTube channels, Facebook lives, IG lives, or in-person events.

You're going to embrace the fear, boldly make the ask, and put yourself out there. If you get a no, you're going to ask someone else. Then someone else. And someone else. Until you get three guest spots.

Be Confident When You Pitch

You can pitch to someone you already know. You can ask your audience for suggestions of who to pitch to (and ask them to connect you if they know the person). You can pitch to podcasts you already listen to. You can go to Facebook groups and ask if you can make a pitch. You can do this in all kinds of ways, but the bottom line is that you're going to show up and *do the thing*.

Now, when you show up, there is such a thing as lazy pitching. We don't do lazy pitching around here. We're not doing this halfheartedly. We're CEOs. We're our own bosses. When you are pitching to be on a podcast, be bold and be clear. State who you are, what problem you solve, and what you'd like to talk about on the podcast.

"My name is Doctor Una. I'm a pediatrician. I help _____ [ideal client that has this problem] get _____ [specific solution]. I would be happy to talk about _____, _____, and _____.

You want this person to immediately think, "Oh my goodness, you're the perfect guest for my show. What time works for you?"

Show up like a boss and pitch yourself with confidence. You want to make yourself THE option. You want to be a category of one. "I'm the person you've been looking for."

You might be thinking to yourself, "I don't want to bother this person. What if they don't need guests? What if they say no?"

Let me tell you something about everybody who does Facebook Lives and podcasts and YouTube interviews. They need high-quality guests every single week. That's not an easy thing to pull off. When you show up and pitch yourself, you're not being a problem. You're a solution to their problem. So you pitch yourself confidently. "I'm the answer you've been looking for." They won't be annoyed or bothered; they'll be relieved and happy.

All of these "what ifs" are just the fear talking, and we're in charge here, not fear.

Start the Snowball Rolling

Appearing as a guest on podcasts and other platforms is how you're going to position yourself as an expert. The more guest spots you do, the more people will see you as an expert. You'll be setting yourself up to be the best option for what you do. You're going to build a business and a brand that is omnipresent. You're going to have people *you don't even know* telling other people to work with you. All because you continuously and relentlessly show up on other people's platforms. So, if we want our brands to grow, our job is putting ourselves in front of people who do not know us. Week after week after week.

I've built a very dominant brand that I'm both proud of and humbled by, but guess what I was doing earlier today? I was a guest on someone else's podcast. I'm relentless about this. This is five years later. Relentless. I'm on other people's podcasts, getting in front of other people's groups. And I'm going to keep doing it indefinitely. Why?

Because it's fun, and it works.

This principle has worked for private practices, direct primary care, speakers, event hosts, product-based businesses, service-based businesses, coaches. It works. Over two hundred doctors in the EntreMD Business School will tell you that it works. We do this, and we patiently wait for the snowball.

The snowball is coming.

Remember, this isn't about taking advantage of people. It's about solving their problem. They want a guest, and you're the guest. You're going to do a high-value interview on their show. You're serving their audience. And you get to be in front of their audience. They serve their audience one way, and you serve them another way. So you're not competing. You're collaborating. It's a win-win situation. Actually, it's a win-win-win, because their audience wins too.

I have a friend who does weight loss for physicians. I do business for physicians. Her audience doesn't decrease because I was on her podcast. In fact, she's doing an even greater service to her audience by offering them something she couldn't give them on her own.

You can do this authentically. You can do this with integrity. But the bottom line is that, the more you do it, the more you create what we call in the EntreMD Business School "the snowball." When the snowball gets rolling, you'll go from pitching to podcasts to people coming to you.

You might get so many offers that you actually have to start turning some down. Would you like to have that problem where you have to turn down guest spots? You'll be able to choose the ones that will give you the biggest return on your time investment. That's a really sweet place to be in, believe me.

At some point in the future, you'll achieve celebrity status in your field because so many people know who you are. Now, does that mean, when you reach that status that the work is over? Of course not. Remember Michelle Obama? But you'll be able to choose what you do, how you do it, and your business will continue to grow by leaps and bounds.

An Encouraging Marketing Tip

As we near the end of this chapter, I want to leave you with something I think you'll find very encouraging. So many times people ask me, "How on earth will I keep thinking of new things to say every single week?"

Ed Mylett is a global speaker, coach, entrepreneur, author, podcast host, etc. etc. etc. And he said something once that I've never forgotten:

"Marketing is not about saying new things to old people; it's about saying old things to new people."

You don't have to think of something new to say every single day. Good marketing is about saying the same thing over and over, but saying it to new people. Marketing is all about *attracting new people.* I'll be blunt here. If you're doing a good job of marketing, you'll be bored sometimes by what you're saying. I don't mean in a bad way. You're saying the same thing over and over again. But new people are hearing it every time.

Please don't make the mistake of thinking, "Oh, wow, I talked about something so impactful and profound, but I can't talk about it again, because I've already said it." How many people heard you say it? How many more people out there need to hear it? Keep saying it. Just get in front of new people each time.

Have you ever had this experience where you're saying something you've been saying for months, then you meet someone who is absolutely blown away by it? And you're thinking, "Why? I didn't say anything revolutionary. I've said this so many times already." But it's revolutionary to them because this is the first time they're hearing it.

When we say something that blows someone's mind, but it just seems like common sense to us, that means we're operating out of our zone of genius. Your zone of genius is where things come so naturally to you that you think it must be common sense to everyone. It's not. You're blowing their minds. And it's a beautiful thing.

I always use the example of Christmas. Churches are full for Christmas services every December without fail. Everyone's going to church. They know what they're going to hear. It's nothing new. Jesus the savior is born. Joy to the world. Every single year. It doesn't change. Yet people still go to hear that same message.

So don't be afraid of repeating yourself. Don't be afraid of owning your message and saying it over and over again. Because you're saying the same old wonderful thing to new people.

Now, of course you might use different stories. You might add some creativity around it. And I hope you do. That's really the ideal way to share not-new information. But it's the same principles.

For as long as EntreMD has existed, I've been sharing the same general message. I will uplevel the way I present it. I add in different stories and testimonials. I get better at delivering it. But, at the core, it's the same thing.

Don't be afraid of repeating yourself.

I believe that the physicians reading this book (you!) are going to be building the most innovative, the most impactful, most profitable businesses in the healthcare space (and outside of it). I'm so excited. I can't wait to be a part of it—or even witness it from afar. I'm totally rooting for you.

Your homework for Chapter 2 is to schedule three interviews/guest spots before you move on to Chapter 3. Don't be intimidated by this. If you're scared, embrace the fear and do it anyway. You can absolutely do it. And you will get better and better at this as you go. You're a doctor. Doctors are over-achievers. We do hard things every day. You've got this. I believe in you. It will be a blast. Mark my words. You'll see.

In the next chapter, I'm going to show you how to get your ideal client to jump at the chance to work with you. Can you imagine?

Head over to www.entremd.com/visiblitybook to download your workbook if you haven't already. Now go book those guest spots, and I'll see you soon!

EBS Student Spotlight: Dr. Brittany Panico

Dr. Brittany Panico is a rheumatologist in Phoenix, Arizona. She attended my Visibility Formula workshop because she wasn't happy with where her career was going, and she was looking for a way to set herself apart from her peers. But the idea of stepping out of her comfort zone was scary to her.

At the time, she and her husband were both working full time as physicians, and they had three children under the age of seven. Where would she find the time for whatever it is she would do next?

But she knew she had to find the time. She was burned out, and something had to change. "I can't live like this," she thought to herself. "I can't be in an environment where my ideas don't matter to my peers, my colleagues." She spun in this hamster wheel every single day thinking, "How can I get myself out of this?"

At the time, she was doing the public service loan forgiveness program, so she set a deadline. When her loans were forgiven, she would be done. "Then I'm going to do what I want with my life," she said, "and that's my gift to myself."

Around that time, she had a close friend who opened his own dermatology practice and helped her see what was possible in her own community. He planted that seed in her mind, then she attended the Visibility Workshop, and decided to join EBS.

"It was perfect timing that I joined EBS while I was preparing for my last year of loan payments," she says, "and used that opportunity to really practice and prepare myself for what I wanted to do next."

She was still employed, so she had some restrictions based on her contract, but she started a Facebook profile and did videos and started building her brand under the guidance of EBS. From there, she became very active on LinkedIn and started building a network of people who would recognize her once she decided to leave.

"I really worked on honing and practicing the skills that we go through in the business school," she says. "There are not very many of us that do 100% of the work in EBS. If you work full time, part time, whatever, a lot of us will do 30%. I really laid low and didn't engage very much in the beginning—but I did the work behind the scenes and I paid attention and I listened to what my classmates were doing."

She built up a data bank of information and strategies, did the work, and filed it away until her loans were forgiven and she could open her own practice. She's in a unique position where she joined two nurse practitioners to build an even bigger practice right away. They're independent in her state and collectively became a group. That's how it evolved for her.

"I have the tools that have allowed me to be confident in building this vision that's bigger than what I could have ever imagined," she says. "I learned that by surrounding myself with people who shared similar visions and goals. Those people were far more important than the ones that were holding me back, and it really allowed me to separate myself from my colleagues who didn't want to change."

She's so grateful for the collaboration in EBS. She and her fellow students talk about different ways to build a business that fits your needs and how to use the collective ideas of others to build something really amazing. "I think, too," she says, "that the more lives that I do, the more podcasts I go on, the more conversations I have with people, it's really opened me up to being able to pivot in my own career, my own practice, and think, 'Why am I not offering this to people? Why am I holding back if I can offer this other service and potentially bill for it?'"

It has been so freeing for her to develop great ideas and realize that she doesn't need corporate approval to be able to implement them. She can just decide she wants to do it and run with it. One of her recent ideas led her to meet with a founder of a tech company to discuss building an app for remote monitoring for rheumatology patients. This is the first time she has had the courage and confidence to believe that she's a thought leader in her field and can be the one to come up with a solution for her patients and make a difference in their lives. She just put out a call on LinkedIn and other platforms asking, "Who out there can connect me to somebody who can help me make this a reality?"

Her fellow students in EBS gave her the support and encouragement and confidence to do some really daring things she wouldn't have done in the past. She responds to posts now instead of staying silent. She confidently uses her voice on platforms that used to intimidate her.

"I think a lot of us think Dr. Una is speaking directly to us and it's true," she says. "I was an introverted introvert— just like her. I'm so much more comfortable as a listener and a lurker, but I've learned through her and through EBS just how much I can accomplish if I take those challenges and really try to practice these tools. It's such a powerful network of helping each other realize what we're capable of."

The beauty of this, she says, is that just when you think you've reached a new level, there's another level to aim for. Just like medicine is muscle memory to her now, the business stuff is starting to become that for her too. She's constantly asking, "What are my gaps?" and reaching for business books to listen to on her commute, so she can learn the thing that will take her to that next level.

The students in EBS, she says, are all at different levels of their careers and building businesses "and I think it's just so powerful that we come together and help each other meet those goals and really celebrate those successes, but then help each other through those troughs. We've had classmates who are very vulnerable in expressing their struggles and, collectively, people have come up with ideas that help them through that.

It's so powerful to be able to be in a community that literally is no judgment. It's all about how we can be better together."

Dr. Panico says EBS gave her the courage to leave a place where she did not feel valued. "Rather than being a cog in the wheel, I decided my voice is different and I no longer align with the values of this organization."

She remembers someone in one of the EBS classes saying that "during a negotiating phase, no is a complete sentence." So when she sat down with her boss to give her resignation, he looked at her and said, "I'd like you to reconsider what you're saying," and she said, "No thank you. I envision my career going in a different direction and I'm here to let you know that I will no longer be here 90 days from now. I'm giving you my resignation."

Dr. Panico knows that physicians are people pleasers—because we're helpers and caretakers—but we can learn to let go of that when it's not serving us. We don't have to let others persuade us to change our minds. "We are the authority," she says. "We're the authority of what's in our heads. Just being at a place where I feel I can stand up for myself—knowing that I'm worth the ideas I have and decisions I make—I can't even put a price tag on that feeling of empowerment."

She says she's a different person now. Her new mindset has allowed her to take chances in other areas of her life where she'd been holding back because she thought other people wanted something different from her. "That doesn't matter anymore," she says. "It's what

I want for myself and my family and what I envisioned my career to be like."

She says you need the support of the EBS community to live your dream life, "because the rest of the world doesn't necessarily feel that way. They're not feeling your vision, so when you have that safe place where you can be yourself and you can be vulnerable and where you can tell fear to take a back seat, it's absolutely priceless.

Dr. Panico went on to launch her practice and within six months her schedule was fully booked and she needed to hire another clinician. When asked about this, she said it's unfathomable what can happen when you invest in yourself.

CHAPTER 3:

How to Get Your Ideal Client to Jump at the Opportunity to Work With You

When I do the Visibility Formula workshop in real time, I get to experience transformations as they happen. I get to watch people set up interviews, tweak their websites, own their voice, celebrate victories big and small. I can't tell you how excited it makes me.

I don't get that same privilege when I write a book. I write the book at one point in time, and you read it at another. But I'm excited for you and inspired by you just the same. I believe in you just the same. I know you're experiencing transformation, and I hope I get to hear about it someday. And I hope you're ready for this chapter, because it's going to be so much fun.

This chapter will be a little bit different than Chapters 1 and 2. With those, I pretty much dove right into the meat of the chapter from the beginning. For this one, I'm going to take some time to set the stage. You'll see why when we get to the part about your HQ (stay with me here).

As promised in the chapter title, I'm going to tell you how to set the stage for your ideal client to jump at the opportunity to work with you. But first I'll set the stage for why this is one of the most important things you'll ever do in your business.

Let's Keep the Momentum Going

I want to take a moment to think about everything you've already accomplished so far as you've read this book. I want you to think about what life could look like as you continue to live in this momentum. This is the same thing that other people are using to create some incredibly transformational movements in their businesses and in their lives. We're physicians, so we're going to build good systems around it, and we're going to do so much good in the world.

Even if you pitched a lot of people and haven't gotten a yes yet, you've put yourself out there (which is huge), and it's only a matter of time before you start hearing "yes yes yes!" You're giving it your best shot, and I'm so proud of you.

This book is experiential. I want you to experience true transformation in your business and your life. Are you tired of reading and taking courses and just stockpiling more and more information? We want to learn new things, sure, but with this book, we're reading to *do*, not reading to *know*. We've already got a lot of knowledge.

We're reading this book in order to take action. We want to learn the things we need to know, to do the things we need to do, to get the results we want to get.

Like I've said (but it bears repeating as a pep talk), I started off my entrepreneurial journey as a super shy, socially awkward, introverted introvert with no business education, terrified of talking about money, terrified of putting myself out there. So I understand everything you're going for, and I'm on your side. I'm your evidence that it doesn't matter where you're starting from, you can do this. You're putting yourself out there, and it's going to pay off.

It is absolutely going to pay off.

In this chapter, we're going to have a blast. We're going to talk about how to set the stage to get people to want to work with you. Do you want more patients? More clients? Do you want more, more, more?

Wanting more is not greed. Wanting more is a good thing, a healthy thing. Because what do we do in our businesses? We serve people. We help them solve problems. We take away their pain. We do good stuff as entrepreneurs. Wanting more means we solve more problems and serve more people.

Whether your business is just an idea in your head at this point, or you've already hit multiple seven figures, these classic strategies will always work. In the EntreMD world, we're not into fads. We're not into things that come and go. We deal in classic strategies here. It literally doesn't matter what the algorithms are doing. It doesn't matter if there's a recession or not.

These are things that work. Every time.

If you're just starting out, these things will help you build a solid foundation that will last. If you already have a business, these things will help you to continue to build that foundation even as you uplevel more and more. This isn't a thing where, once you cross a certain threshold, you outgrow it. I am a student of business. I watch some of the most successful businesses very closely and study them very carefully. They are still doing this stuff after years and years of success.

It's important to understand that I want to help doctors build businesses in such a way that they're also building a dominant brand alongside it. This way, whatever you end up doing in the future, you have the brand to support it. So you become an opportunity magnet. For now, you might be thinking your thing is private practice, but you don't know what's coming down the road. If you have a dominant brand, you'll be ready for it when it comes. Whatever it is—even if you can't see it right now—you'll be ready for it.

Last year, I was happily working hard to build EntreMD, and someone came to me, "I'm looking to sell my company. With what you're doing, I think it would be a perfect fit for you." So even though it was not on my vision board to purchase a company last year, I purchased a company. What set the stage for that? My dominant brand.

It opens these doors for amazing opportunities I never could have envisioned.

We're Keeping It Simple. Always.

As with all things always in EntreMD, the strategies we're going to be talking about will be simple. But don't be confused by the simplicity of it. My agenda is to take business principles and demystify them, to make them simple. So they're simple but they're profound. They're simple, but they've created unbelievable results for people.

Do you like simple? I do. So many people start businesses and then quit before they even get them off the ground. And it's often because they're overwhelmed. Everything feels complicated and complex. No, starting a business isn't easy. But it doesn't have to be complicated. There are so many ways to keep it simple, keep it working.

From the beginning, we've talked about becoming known for what you do. You have this thing that you're known for. That's what we did in Chapter 1.

In Chapter 2, now that you've decided what you want to be known for, how do we take that message that you have and put it everywhere?

And here we are in Chapter 3. Now that you've put yourself out there and people are thinking, "Oh, this person is amazing," how do we set the stage so they follow you back and then decide to work with you?

I don't think anyone reading this book just wants to collect a lot of fans and no clients or patients, right? That's aborting the process halfway. We don't just want admirers; we want people to sign up to work with us. We want to bring it full circle. We want to bring them home. We want to help them; we want to serve them; we want to do all of that.

And we don't just *want* to do it. *We're going to do it.*

Let's Paint a Picture

You know I always try to get us in the right frame of mind when we talk about big things like this, so I want you to indulge me and do something. For the next 30 seconds, I want you to close your eyes and imagine that you've built your business and, in your industry, you've become known for what you do. Just think about that. Paint that picture. You're known for what you do, and you've built a business that's omnipresent so people know you. People know about you. When people say, "I have this problem," your name comes up. Think about that.

Got it? Okay, now I want you to think about all the people who know you. You have all the clients and patients you want. And you've created this business that has given you financial freedom; it's given you time freedom; it's given you so much satisfaction because you're doing such meaningful work.

It's almost as if you're doing what you were born for.

Once you see that picture, say out loud, "I see it." Because what we're going to talk about in the pages ahead, we'll be doing with that picture top of mind. The Imagination Police aren't welcome here, so feel free to dream big. Can you see it?

Once upon a time, you were a pimply teenager who made the decision in front of the family that you wanted to be a doctor, and you did it. If you did that, then you can do this. We're doctors; we do hard things.

So, with that picture, now we're going to work on how to set the stage. How do I get to the place where all these people want to work with me?

Become Google-able and Binge-able

Have you ever listened to a new-to-you podcast or heard a speaker at an event, liked what they were saying, and immediately Googled them to find out more? What happened when you typed their name into Google? Did a whole bunch of great content come up, or were you disappointed (even ticked) because you couldn't really find anything at all? So you just closed Google and that was the end of it.

Don't be the person who can't be Googled.

You do not want this to happen to you. You do not want to speak at an event, then have someone Google you and find absolutely nothing. What a waste.

No, you're going to go out there and put yourself out in front of other people's audiences. Hopefully you've already started doing it. But you want to make yourself Googleable. You want to make yourself bingeable. When they listen to you one time, you want them to head to Google, and find out that there is a ton of your stuff for them to catch up on.

For better or worse, we live in a binge economy. Think about Netflix. You go on Netflix and find a new show and the new season has two episodes. I don't know about you, but I don't start watching a show that only has two episodes released. That's a complete waste of time. I'll come back when there's a whole season (or two or three) for me to watch all at once.

When people find out about you and Google you, you want to have a place where they can come and just sit with you for a long time, soaking you up. And the whole time they're sitting with you, you're solving their problems, because that's what your content does. You're solving their problem; they're seeing people you've worked with; and the entire time, they're making their way toward the ultimate decision: "This is the person I want to work with."

This is why, when you're first starting to create content, and it feels like you're not getting very many eyes on your videos (or ears on your podcast), you don't worry about it. You keep going. You keep producing and releasing great content, week in and week out. Because the day will come when people start to catch on. You'll be on someone's podcast and one or two or ten people will Google you to find out more, and you'll have 40 or 140 podcast episodes for them to listen to.

And there's your snowball. I'm telling you, it's magical.

It's Time to Set Up an HQ

You might be thinking, "Hold on, Dr. Una. I don't have a podcast or a blog or a YouTube channel. How am I going to become bingeable?"

You're going to start one.

Yes, you read that right. You're going to set up your own personal headquarters on the internet. In EBS, we call this your HQ. If you want to be bingeable, you need to have a place for people to land when they Google you. It could be a podcast, a YouTube channel, a blog.

Now, let me be clear about this. I'm not talking about a Facebook page, an Instagram account, a TikTok, or any other social media platform. Yes, those are great to have, and you should do any/all of them that are a good fit for you and your business. But they are a spin-off, not the main deal.

Why? Because, sadly, social media is owned by someone who is *not* you, and your account could literally disappear at any moment if you get banned or the platform gets shut down or goes away. I know people who have had accounts with 35k followers,

80k followers, and they lost them overnight. What a nightmare.

Your HQ is yours. You own it. It's a place to house your content that's yours, that belongs to you, that you have complete control over, that no one can ban or shut down or take away. You really don't want to spend years building something on someone else's property. That's dangerous. I'm all for taking risks, but not that kind of risk.

So you need an HQ—a podcast, a YouTube channel, or a blog. Now, your brain might automatically go to "I don't know how to do that. I'm not tech-savvy. I can't do any of those kinds of things." But I want you to hear me. Don't let your brain go there. Tell your brain to chill for a minute. We're not going to talk about the technical aspect of it quite yet. That's actually the easiest part.

Remember, you memorized the Krebs cycle. You can learn to launch a YouTube channel or podcast. We're doctors here. We've done hard things. Okay? We're not going to let that thought distract us.

When you set up an HQ (a podcast, YouTube channel, blog), this becomes your legacy body of work. For instance, we're on episode 387 of the EntreMD podcast as I write these words (it will be a whole lot more when you read them). I want you to think about that. Three plus years of podcasting 1-2 times a week. The first year it was once a week, now 2x a week. That's my body of work.

You cannot outbinge me. I have almost 400 episodes under my belt. It will take you more than a few weekends to get through all of that. You're giving people a no-pressure opportunity to explore and explore and see what you're all about and decide if they want to work with you.

It's like the samples at Costco that they hand out for free to get you to buy their food in bulk. You're giving people a little taste of what you can do for them. You're letting them try you before they say yes to working with you. You're letting them date you before they say absolutely yes I will marry you.

People listen to the EntreMD podcast; they get wins in their business; and they think, "I'm getting all these wins just by listening to the podcast. What would it be like to join the EntreMD Business School?"

I'm not spending valuable time having a one-on-one conversation with them. They're having a conversation in their house at 2am while I'm sleeping—all because I took the time to build a body of work they could binge on their own time.

So, besides being your legacy, your podcast or YouTube channel is like an employee that works for you 24/7 and you're not paying them. How many of you would like to have this full-time employee who works 24/7 and doesn't get burnt out, doesn't complain, and doesn't come to work late? What a great employee, right?

One of our EBS alumni just celebrated a million downloads on YouTube. When you hear about someone who has a million downloads on YouTube, what comes to mind? Expert. Thought leader. Must know what she's talking about. Should be the speaker at my event. It establishes you as the authority.

Getting your content out there is how you establish yourself as a thought leader. This book is another example of that. I write it once; I put it out in the world; I tell people about it; then I let it work for me. I don't know when you're reading it, but it could be weeks, months, years after I wrote it. It's a full-time employee of mine that I don't even have to pay. Beautiful.

So we want to have an HQ where our content lives. There's absolutely no reason not to. And every reason in the world to make it happen.

Make Your HQ Profitable by Creating Wins for You and Your Client

So let's talk about the strategy a little bit, because the last thing you want to do is to have a YouTube channel or a podcast or a blog, and it's a total waste of time from an entrepreneur's perspective. You've got to make it profitable.

Two things should be happening with your HQ:

1. It should be creating a win for your client-to-be.
2. It should be creating a win for you.

We do things in pairs in EntreMD. We serve *and* we earn. We do both. We create a win-win situation for our clients and ourselves. Both people should be winning. That's what makes this a beautiful symbiotic relationship, not a parasitic relationship.

So how do you create wins for your clients? You solve problems. Your clients have questions. In your content, you answer them. For example, when I did a weekly show for my private practice, the parents had a lot of questions. Now, some of those questions seemed really basic to me. (Example: My child's poop is green. Is this normal?)

But guess what. It's not about me. It's about my clients. What do they need? They have questions. They want to know if things are normal or not. They want reassurance that their kid is going to be okay. You're the expert. You have the knowledge and information they need. They trust you to provide them with answers. There are myths out there that they might believe. In your content, you debunk those myths. This is how you serve them right where they are.

They're wondering, "Is this the person I should work with?" In your content, you establish that. You establish that by showing your authority and by sharing your clients'/patients' wins. You share those glowing testimonials and people think, "Huh, I bet I could get that result too."

In addition to answering questions, you can solve problems by sharing how-tos. I do a lot of that on the EntreMD podcast. Physician entrepreneurs don't know how to do something and they want to know. Things like:

- How to make your first $1M in revenue.
- How to think like someone building a 7-figure business.
- How to convert your payroll expenses to an investment.
- How to choose the right coach for you.
- How to sell without selling.

They want to know these things. They're googling it already. Be the trusted answer they're looking for.

Answering questions, debunking myths, mindset shifts, testimonials—all of that is win-win content. This is bingeable content. You're solving timeless problems so your people go back over and over and over again, any time that problem comes back up in their lives.

You want people listening to you and saying, "It's like you're in my head. That's the question I've been asking. How did you know? This is exactly what I needed to hear." That's what your content should be doing—creating wins. Even while you sleep.

Don't Be Afraid of Giving Away Your Best Stuff

The advice I'm going to give you in this section might be a little controversial. I can see why that might be, but it shouldn't be.

Don't be afraid of giving away your best stuff.

Earlier this year, I offered the four-day Visibility Formula workshop for FREE. I asked the attendees what they would have paid for it. The answers ranged from $299 to $10,000. And you're getting that same goodness in a $15 book.

This isn't fluff. I'm not just throwing meaningless things at you because you paid so little for it. Not at all. I don't do fluff. This is my best stuff. I want this to be better than the last few things you paid big money for. I want you to shake your head and say, wow, she packed it all in there. I literally am holding nothing back.

Somebody reading this book right now (maybe you) is thinking, "If I could make this level of transformation just reading a $15 book, I want to be in the speed lane. I want to get things done. What would it be like to actually *work* with Dr. Una in the EntreMD Business School?"

And the truth of the matter, at the end of the day, is that someone who works with me for a year—compared to someone who just attended my four-day workshop or read my book—is going to be different. So very different.

Speaking of EBS, my students in the business school came to my workshop as well. I told them they would learn a lot. I intended to make it so valuable that even the people who spend time with me every week will find value in it. And they did.

I give away my best stuff. And I'm still building a multi-million dollar business, giving away my best stuff. Don't be afraid to give away your best stuff. Seriously.

Don't think to yourself, "I'm just going to give them the beginner stuff and hide the rest." Don't do that. You're a thought leader. Thought leaders lead with their thoughts.

So that's the win for the client. They're getting a whole lot of value for free. But the second win is for you. Don't fall into the trap of saying "But I just want to help people." Of course you do. And you will. The best way you can help people is to create a win-win for both of you. If you want your business to stay in business, you have to be profitable.

A win isn't enough. We need both. A win-win.

Leverage a Call to Action

The part that helps *you* is what makes some doctors uncomfortable. But remember, we talked about fear in Chapter 1. And we decided that we were not going to let fear stop us. We made that decision already, and we're sticking with it no matter what.

The win for you is leveraging a call to action. With your content, you are helping people and you are inviting them to work with you. Don't be afraid to invite people to work with you.

Depending on your business, a call to action can be:

- Come to my practice.
- Join my coaching program.
- I can help you with x, y, or z.

When you make this call to action, you need to understand that, as an entrepreneur, you solve problems. You are not manipulating people. You are not trying to swindle people and steal their money. You are not a fraudster. You are not a greedy doctor.

You are somebody who helps people.

We live in an economic world where there is always a transaction, an exchange. So, if you help people, people will say "thank you." And the thank you note is called money. It's as simple as that. I talk a lot about the importance of getting comfortable around money — talking about it, asking for it, accepting it. It's literally a piece of mercury paper with dead men's faces on it. That's all it is.

We must get comfortable inviting people to work with us because we are solving problems. We're offering a service someone wants and needs. Somewhere out there your ideal client is looking for you. They have a problem; they are aware of it; they want the solution; they are willing; and they are able to pay. You are not manipulating people when you invite them to work with you. They are looking for you.

They want you.

You get it. I know you do. How many times have you had a problem in your life where you were actively looking for somebody to make that problem go away? You might even have put out a call—can somebody, anybody show me where this person is who can help me? And you were ready to pay them. You most likely have a problem like this right now.

I know a lot of doctors who are excited about the idea of entrepreneurship but hate the idea of selling. If what you have to offer people has value to them, is something they really need, why would you not want to sell it to them? Why would you hold it back? Selling isn't deceptive or sleazy. It's communicating with clarity and passion about how you can help someone solve a problem they have.

You're not a sleazy car salesman. You're a matchmaker. Someone has a problem and they want it to go away. You have the solution and you'd like to be paid to work on it for this person. Boom. A match made in heaven. That's it.

Some people are not going to say yes, and that's okay. You don't have to be afraid of rejection. They're not rejecting *you*. It's just not the right fit or the right timing. It's not a perfect match. But the perfect matches are out there. Remember, every ideal client you'll ever need exists right now.

And you're going to find them and keep leveraging that call to action until you get every yes you need and want. You want to make sure you include a call to action in every piece of content you create. This is the number one mistake I see in content creation. There's no call to action to help your audience figure out what to do next. It's absolutely essential, and you can't leave it out.

Don't be afraid. Don't be ashamed. Lean into the fact that you solve problems and you live in an economic world. That's just the way it works. You're solving their problem, and they're willing and able to pay.

And you deserve to be paid.

Three Objections that Will Inevitably Come Up

When you've been doing this for as long as I have, you pretty much have all possible objections memorized. I don't mind objections. I get it. It's human nature. We're naturally skeptical until there's enough proof to change our minds.

If you're reading this book, you know there's more out there for you. Your objections are more along the lines of: please assure me that I can do this and it's all going to turn out fine.

Here are three of the biggest objections I get when I tell people they'll need to set up an HQ for their business:

#1: I will run out of content.

"I don't want to start a YouTube channel and put weekly content out there, because I'll run out of things to say," they tell me.

My rebuttal: As long as you have the three healthy obsessions we talked about in Chapter 1, you cannot possibly run out of content. It is literally impossible. If you're only thinking about yourself, then of course you'll run out of content, because you have to constantly imagine more and more. You have to pull it out of your own brain, your own imagination. Yes, that well can run dry.

But, if your focus is your ideal client, the pain they have, and the outcome you can give them—if serving them is your obsession—you cannot and will not run out of content.

Do you want some podcast episode ideas? Here are some:

- How to convert your podcast into a client attraction machine.
- What If I Run Out of Content?
- What to Do If You Feel Embarrassed Asking People to Work with You

Do you see what I mean? I take my potential clients' questions and concerns and make podcast episodes about them. As long as I'm obsessed with serving my ideal client, I will never, ever run out of content. As long as I'm thinking about YOU, I can't run out. As soon as I flip the focus and start thinking/worrying about myself, that's when I'll run out of content.

I can create content around the questions they're asking, the obstacles they're facing, the things that are stopping them, the anxieties and fears that keep them up at night, the myths that are getting in their way.

For instance, I'm in the business world, and there's talk of a recession and the great resignation. Here are some ideas for YouTube videos:

- How to recession-proof your business.
- How to hire in the midst of the great resignation.
- Top five employee retention strategies.

As long as you're thinking about your people, you cannot run out of content. It is impossible.

#2: I have a successful 7-figure business and I haven't done any of this.

If this is you, and you're reading this book, you must be curious about how to get more eyes on your business, right? Why else would you pick up a book about the Visibility Formula?

So let me ask you a question: What could your business look like if you were doing it? What is the opportunity cost of not doing it? If you were a thought leader, would you have to work less to get people through your doors? If you were a thought leader, would it be easier to attract an A team? If you were a thought leader, could you be an opportunity magnet? What opportunities could land in your lap, but they can't right now, because people can't find you?

So, even if you've built a business, and it's worked so well, when you add all of this, it turns everything around.

Everything I'm teaching in this book is absolutely for any physician just starting out as an entrepreneur. And it's also for everyone who is an established entrepreneur building a multi-seven figure company. I want you to realize that there are times of plenty and then there are times like now when we're in a recession. You want to build a business that can survive in the good times and in the bad times. Which means that you're building a business where, if you have these things in place, and things go south, you can dial them all the way up and you'll be fine.

So don't take the easy route of saying, "Oh, we're okay without doing all of these things." Embrace them all. Because when things happen, you want to have Plan B, Plan C, Plan D.

What have you got to lose?

#3: I can't do this.

Of course you can do this. You went to medical school. You memorized the Krebs Cycle. You replace knees. You replace hearts. You intubate 1kg babies. You save lives. Of course you can do this. If anyone can do this, it's physicians.

If you need me to, I'll believe in you until you can believe in yourself. I've seen hundreds and hundreds of physician success stories over the past few years, and every single one of them started out at least a little bit afraid. And now they're killing it.

You can do this. You can do this. You can do this. End of story.

Choose Your HQ

Okay, it's go time. We're not going to put this off another minute. You know everything you need to know to get started. Which platform will you choose as the landing spot, the headquarters, for all of your amazing content? What's your HQ?

- podcast
- YouTube channel
- blog

Back in the day, I would have chosen a blog, because I was an introvert, and that was the least intimidating way of doing it. If you choose a blog as your HQ, make sure it's because you genuinely believe it will be the most effective. Don't choose it because you're scared of being on video.

Pick one and own it. Head over to www.entremd. com/visiblitybook to download your workbook if you haven't already. Don't start reading the next chapter until you've done your homework for this one. They build on each other.

Now you might be thinking, "How am I going to start a podcast on top of everything else I'm trying to do right now?"

What a great question. I'm so glad you asked. In the next chapter, I'm going to show you how to build a system so that you can do these things consistently—but in less time. That's the dream, right? Working smarter, not harder.

Put these strategies from Chapter 4 in place and, before you know it, your business will be a well-oiled machine.

EBS Student Spotlight: Dr. Diana Mercado-Marmarosh

Dr. Diana Mercado-Marmarosh is a family medicine physician and ADHD coach for physicians and healthcare professionals. "Prior to EBS, COVID really did a number on many of us." she says. "For me, the reality hit that the 200-300 open charts and my graveyard of unfinished business was not something that was sustainable." She thought something was wrong with her. "I used to wonder why I could be a physician but I couldn't keep my house orderly or be on time for my patients."

During COVID, she realized that something had to change. "I started to invest in coaching and, while things were getting a little bit better, I realized that I had to stop ignoring my own ADHD and that I had to invest in that part of it so that I could come to understand myself."

She had always been too embarrassed and ashamed to tell anyone that she had ADHD. "Now I scream it at the top of my lungs," she says, "and every time I diagnose somebody with ADHD, I'm like 'Congratulations! You have ADHD!' and they look at me like I'm crazy. But I've come to realize that ADHD is a gift. You just have to learn how to unwrap it."

Until recently, entrepreneurship wasn't on her mind at all. She assumed she'd always be working a 9-5 job and not have to worry about the business side of it. She just thought she'd show up and her patients would be there, and she wouldn't need to know anything about marketing or any of that.

Prior to joining EBS in June 2021, she had just completed her training to be a life coach and had one $2k launch under her belt. She realized she needed to start completing some challenges, putting herself out there, marketing, explaining to people why they needed a life coach.

By January 2023, she had launched her 10th coaching group and had helped 90 medical students, physicians, and other healthcare professionals. And she's still practicing full time. At the end of her first year in EBS, she had made $138k from her coaching business.

She has learned so much about ADHD and how it can affect entrepreneurs. "We can talk about mindset until we're blue in the face," she says, "but you've got to have systems in place. You don't know what you don't know. Most of us are willing to work hard—that's the only thing that we've known our whole life. But the systems that got us here are not going to be the systems that get us to our next phase."

She speaks to the importance of having a team that will support you so you can work at your highest level. "And delegation, for somebody with ADHD," she says, "was not something that was easy for me to do. I learned that those of us with ADHD have low dopamine and most of us don't want to give ourselves a break because we think we haven't earned it. But when we take frequent breaks and do things we enjoy, we're actually more efficient."

With a full-time job and two small children, you can only do so much. "But I started going to Dr. Una's retreats," she says, "and did probably 30% of her challenges. Those challenges helped me establish myself as a leader and now I speak at conferences that I only dreamed of attending."

She has presented at the ADHD conference and the Texas Medical Association, and she just got an invitation to speak in Rome on mental health.

She has come a long way from her first launch when she didn't even know how to use Zoom or how to charge people. She shares these things to encourage others that anything is possible, even if you're starting with zero business or tech knowledge. She learned how to use Zoom and Paypal but says she still doesn't know how to use Instagram because she delegated that one right off the bat.

"I've had a podcast for a year now," she says, "and I don't know how the magic happens behind the thing, I just get on a call and I talk to amazing people and then I send that over to my virtual assistant to edit it."

She says that every one of us can learn these things. All business skills are learnable. "Business is fun but it's also hard if you don't have the right community. Having the right community is the shortcut." She says that the EBS community is so collaborative, and it has spoiled her. She recently reached out to someone who wasn't in EBS to ask a question, and the person said they didn't want to help her. "What if you take off and become better than me?" they asked. That would never happen in EBS.

"You need to bet on yourself," she says. "Be willing to put in the work and trust yourself. You become your best investment and you keep trying different things." She started asking herself: "What if I can work smarter instead of harder and lean on the community?" She recognizes the EBS network as her net worth because of the people in the room with connections that can open so many doors for you.

Last year she hosted an international retreat for physicians in Costa Rica, providing CME and letting them know they could level up their executive and function and emotional regulation tools and relationships. "Never in my wildest dreams would I have thought that would be something that would be possible," she says, "but here I am doing it."

And this is just her side hustle (that's bringing in six figures). She's still working full time, but she has rearranged her schedule to align with everything else she's doing. "At the beginning, I would have never thought that I could ask for a day off," she says. Then she went down to a 4-day week for 18 months. Now she only works Wednesdays, Thursdays, and Fridays from 7a-7p. And her pay still increases every year.

She did step down from a couple positions (including Chief Medical Officer) because she decided she "wanted to play more." She is more present with her family on Saturdays and Sundays. And she uses Mondays and Tuesdays to "go even more all in" on her coaching business and "seek more opportunities."

CHAPTER 4:

How to Build a System for Simple and Consistent Marketing in Less Time

So we've talked about finding your ideal clients, becoming known for something, building a dominant brand, guest speaking on podcasts and other platforms, maintaining your HQ, becoming a thought leader and the number one go-to person in your industry.

Besides excitement, what comes to mind when you think of all these things? I know what comes to mind for me: *where am I going to find the time?*

What if I could show you a way that you could get all of that done in a fraction of the time? Does that sound like something you'd like to know?

That's what this chapter is all about. In this chapter we're going to learn how to build a system so we can do all the things we've been talking about in a consistent way, a systematic way, so that your ideal client is like, "You are the only option."

We're going to look at some of the keys to building your dream business and living your dream life *at the same time*. People think they have to work really hard now and then later they have their dream life. No, you can do both. Whatever your dream life is, there's a seed version you can live right now. It won't be the whole thing to the fullest extent, but you can definitely start. And that seed version is bigger and better than you think.

This is one of those things that people pay thousands of dollars to learn about, but I'm giving it to you here for the price of this book. Why? Because I love physicians, and I want us to win.

What We've Learned So Far

In the first chapter, we looked at how to become known for what you do. And we got that. We have one thing and we're going to own that thing. We're going to show up, we're going to own our voices, we're going to become a thought leader in that space. When people think about the problem we solve, they'll think about us.

In the second chapter, now that we're clear on what our one thing is, now that we're no longer confused, how are we going to amplify that? First of all, we came to this very amazing discovery that everybody we will ever need to serve already exists, and we learned how to put ourselves in front of them. And you guys went on to do the things—get booked on podcasts, etc. You made the decision to put yourself out there in front of your ideal person.

In chapter three, okay, now I've put myself out there, so how do I set the stage? You decided on an HQ— YouTube channel, podcast, or blog—to create or uplevel. We've built this web, so when they come, they just want to stay because we have become bingeable. Our content will work for us even when we're not working.

These principles I'm teaching you in this book are the same ones I use in my business. If you look at the data, only 2% of businesses owned by female founders cross the $1M mark. Crossing the $2M mark twice makes us a 1% company. They're the same principles I used to publish two best-selling books. The same principles we used to create a 1% podcast. It's all the same principles.

Do We Really Need an HQ?

Do we really need an HQ, a place where our body of work can live for a long time, even after we're gone? We absolutely do.

As physicians, we have some of the best experiences, the greatest expertise, the greatest stories. We have a heart for humanity. We love to help people. Our voices are needed. That legacy body of work will continue to work for you 24/7, even after you're gone. It will continue to serve the ones who come after you, and it will bless the family you've left behind.

Two days ago I was listening to someone who died 12 years ago. His legacy lives on. My mind was blown. The guy is dead, but he's still touching my life, because he took the time to build a body of work. When you're building it, it won't look like much, but as time goes on, it compounds.

I've only been doing my podcast for 3.5 years and we already have 387 episodes, over 600k downloads, and thousands and thousands of lives touched. People tell me all the time that my podcast has affected their life in a positive way. And we're only three years in. What happens in year 7? What happens in year 10? What happens in year 15? What happens after I'm gone?

Own your voice. Own your legacy body of work.

Just Take that Next Step

If you've been following me for any length of time, you've probably heard me reference Brian Tracy's book, *Eat That Frog*. It's all about how to stop procrastinating and get more done in less time. But it's also a great motivator when you're feeling overwhelmed, afraid, or maybe both of those at once.

People often think there are these really dramatic things you need to do to create quantum leaps in your business. There aren't. It's all about just getting started, taking the next step, then the next. Keep doing that week after week, and it compounds. Before you know it, snowball!

Think about the wins you've already created in your business since you started reading this book (as long as you've actually done the homework assignments, that is). Imagine the wins you'll create if you just keep going.

If you read my book, *The EntreMD Method*, you know how I started my podcast. It was just like, "Hey, yeah, we should start a podcast." I didn't know how to do it, but I did it anyway. I used my iPhone and AirPods. "Welcome to the first episode of the EntreMD podcast. I'm in my basement!"

In a little over a month, I went from no podcast to more than a thousand downloads. Eighteen months later, my podcast had more than one hundred thousand downloads." It wasn't perfect, but I decided to shoot for excellence and keep perfecting it along the way. Failures are just part of the process on the way to success.

With doctors, our fear of failure can lead to perfectionism. How can we get past that? We can focus on excellence, not perfection. Excellent work is the best work you can produce at the time with the knowledge and resources at your disposal. Aim for excellence and start taking action today. This is one of the superpowers of the ultra successful. Don't wait. Tomorrow is not a better day than today. Start today, and each day after that you'll just keep getting better and better and better.

That's literally how my podcast started. I did the best I could, but I was nowhere near perfect. I didn't have to be. You don't have to be either. If you see any results that I get, and it's in any way inspiring to you, that's how it's been done. Think of people you admire. That's how they're getting it done too.

So you're going to feel the fear and do it anyway. And how will you get to the next level? Just find the next step and take it. You never know where it will lead. But it will be so good. Because you're following your dreams.

It doesn't matter if you're just starting. It doesn't matter if you've crossed the seven-figure mark. There's something ahead of you that maybe you've held back on dreaming of. Give yourself permission to dream.

Go For Your Dreams

Do you want a dream business and a dream life? You can have them both. I do. A few years ago, I gave myself permission to dream, and I haven't looked back.

Here's the thing. As physicians, we've been sold a lie. We can't do it. We're one-trick ponies. We should stay in our lane. Let the business people handle business. No, we're not doing that anymore. We can dream whatever we want. We can live life and practice medicine on our terms.

For me, a big part of living life on my terms is building a business where I don't have to sacrifice my family or the relationships that matter most to me. I want a business AND a life.

For example, I decided a few years ago that one thing I really wanted to do was to homeschool my older kids (I can't teach little people). So I homeschool my 15-year-old and my 14-year-old. And I drive my two younger kids to and from school. I wanted to take time off from my practice, so I took a 24-month sabbatical. In 24 months, I have not stepped foot in my practice, and it has grown. Grown.

I also decided I wanted to follow my dream of being a mentor to a lot of people, people who can not afford to work with me. Remember, business and charity are separate. And I do that. I mentor hundreds of people because that's what I want to do. I am living life on my own terms.

You, too, can build a dream business and create a dream life at the exact same time. You can learn how to do it. You can pay the price for it and do the work so you can have it. We're going to work like nobody else, so later we can live like nobody else. But not that much later. It's right after the decision. I'm going to live my dream life *and* have my dream business.

We don't have to follow the paradigm that we see. We don't have to. We can take control. And it doesn't matter that you may be running a private practice and people have told you, "Too bad, you're stuck here." You're not. We can live life and practice medicine on our own terms.

Dr. Tolu is an EBS student who wanted to build her own practice but thought she couldn't. But she did. Eighteen months later, she had 4000 patients. Four thousand patients. And, on top of that, she's been able to work out her schedule so that she can go to her kids' school and have lunch with them. Can you imagine that? In 18 months, you build a practice with 4000 patients and you're chilling, having lunch with your kids a few times a week.

Do you like the sound of that? Maybe her dream is not your specific dream, but she has time to do what she wants. What doctor doesn't want that?

I'm going to give you some practical tips for making your dream a reality. I'm going to share three things you can do to create a system that helps you get more done in less time — and gets you in front of more people consistently. They're not rocket science, but they'll change your life. Those three things are:

1. batching
2. delegation
3. repurposing

Let's go through them one at a time, starting with batching.

Batching Will Change Your Life

Let's say you've decided to start a podcast, and you're going to air weekly episodes. That means that, over the course of a month, you'll need to record four podcast episodes. Let's say a new episode releases every Monday. Here's what I see so many people do:

When they release the new episode on Monday, they breathe a sigh of relief, then immediately start worrying about next week's episode. "I don't know what I'm going to talk about. I'm so worried. And when will I record it? I'm so worried." This internal struggle goes on every single day until you record the next week's episode on Sunday night. You release it on Monday, breathe that quick sigh of relief, and the mental cycle of angst starts right back up all over again.

Stop it.

Do you see how stressful that is? How painful? Not physically painfully, but mentally excruciating. At the very least, you're dealing with way too much unnecessary mental clutter. At worst, you're putting yourself through mental torture. Every single week, all week long. That's no way to live. That's not freedom.

I want you to think about inertia and momentum for a minute. When you start the process of recording, you get into momentum, and then you stop and you wait for the next week. It's start, stop, start, stop. There's no flow.

So the first thing you're going to do that's going to change your life forever (and I literally mean *forever*) is batching. Batching is simply the act of doing something all at once instead of spread over a longer period of time. In this case, batching would look like recording all four podcast episodes in one block of time instead of spreading them out over the whole month.

Let's say, on the first Monday of the month, you have a one-hour block of time on your calendar where you sit down and do four outlines for four podcast episodes. Boom boom boom boom. And then you're done.

Then, on the first Tuesday of the month, you have a two-hour block (three hours if you need it) where you record four 30-minute podcast episodes (or four Youtube videos or write four blog posts). In just three (or four) hours, you're done for the month. In fact, if you do it again the following week, you're done for *two* months. You can take the entire summer off from content creation for your HQ.

You're also giving yourself back all those hours and hours of worrying about your next episode. Batching gives you your life back. And your mental wellbeing. And this is one of those things where the way you do one thing is the way you do everything. You can apply this batching to social media and other things you do for your business as well.

When you are in motion, stay in motion and get it done. As opposed to starting, stopping, starting, stopping, thinking about it, starting, stopping, starting, stopping.

Boom. There. Peace and quiet.

When people think of having to produce content every single week for their HQ, they stress out about it. But you know the secret. You don't have to create new content every week to share new content every week. You create it once, schedule it, and you're done. Drop the daily drama, pick two time slots at the beginning of the month, and that's it.

I don't know about you, but that makes me want to exhale a great big sigh of relief.

There's No Successful Business Without Delegation

The second one is one of my favorite things: delegation. I'm going to talk about it in the context of visibility and content, but you can really apply it to every aspect of your life.

Delegation is something that, for us physicians, is so tough to do. I don't know why. Maybe it's because we tend to be perfectionists. "Nobody can do it like me," we think. And we're right. But, if we're being honest, there are plenty of things in our businesses that can be done well enough by someone else. Perfectionism and micromanagement will do nothing but hold us back.

You might be thinking, "My business isn't making any money yet. I can't afford to delegate." I'm going to push back on that a little bit. No, you might not be able to afford a full-time personal assistant, but you can start small.

I know physician entrepreneurs who are spending hours each week editing their own podcasts. Somebody on Fiverr can do that for you for $10. Stop it.

Those same people tell me, "I'm tired. I'm burned out. This business thing is so exhausting." And I'm like, you can get back two hours of your life every single week with $10. Okay, so some people will charge more. Let's say $20 and run some numbers here.

If your hourly rate is $300, and you spent 2 hours editing a podcast and 2 hours outlining it and recording it, you spent 4 hours on one podcast episode. That's $1200. That's a $1200 podcast episode. Is that really what you intended to do? I mean, think about it. When you play it back, are you thinking, wow, this is a $1200 podcast episode?

What's the opportunity cost there? You were supposed to be doing actual revenue-generating activities. There are activities in your business that you could have done instead. Or you could have spent that time with your family or taking a walk—or a nap.

No more $1200 podcast episodes, okay? Value-wise, you should give someone $1200 of information when they listen, but you don't want to spend that much on a podcast episode. The outlining and recording have to be done by you, but the editing can absolutely be delegated.

You can also delegate your show notes or your YouTube description. When you do your podcast, you can create social media posts from it. (We'll be talking more about repurposing in the next section.) Someone can listen to those and pull them out for you. You don't have to be the one who does it. Somebody can load your content on Descript and boom, pull out a reel.

One of the things we need to realize as physicians is that we have the blessing of high earning power. What that means is that we can buy time. Do you understand what I'm saying? You can use the time yourself or you can buy the time. When you're starting a business, you have the capacity to acquire other people's time to get things done, so you can focus on your highest value tasks.

Now, when you first start your business, you may not be able to pay people to do all of that, but there's some version of it that you can afford. Start from there. Start practicing delegation. Start practicing taking things off your plate. Every week when you do your calendar, your to-do list, ask yourself, "Of all of these things here, which of them should I *not* be doing?"

One of our doctors in EBS loved Canva once upon a time. When she'd spend an hour making one graphic, I'd say to her, "Come on, you just made a $350 graphic. Would you pay someone $350 for the graphic you just made? Delegate that stuff. Pay someone $10 to do it for you." She delegates like a rockstar now.

If you're still thinking, "but nobody can do it like me," you're right. Nobody can do it like you. But remember: they can do it pretty well, and that's good enough. We don't need everybody to do it like you. It's possible they might do it *better* than you.

Focus on your highest value tasks and delegate everything else.

Repurposing Is Magic

The third thing you're going to do to build a system that will streamline your business is repurposing. Repurposing is magic.

Think about nature. There is no seed-bearing tree you see that didn't come from a seed. There are no new trees being created. It was only done once. So the question you've got to ask yourself is this: if I did something once (planted one seed), how can I make a forest out of it?

For instance, if you go to my Instagram page, you'll see a bunch of reels. Let me tell you how all of those reels happened. (Can you keep a secret?) When I go to record my podcast, I flip on my camera and record a video. I do them both at the same time. Then I send the video to my team. They clip it out. They make all these reels. People say, "You're always on social media." I'm not. I do it once, my team takes it and repurposes it. When I create my podcast, it's one thing, but it lives on for a long time, because it's getting repurposed by my team.

Not me, my team.

If you're going to do all of the thinking, the outline, and the recording of your podcast, why would you do it once, then throw it away? Repurpose it.

If you speak at an event and they'll give you the video, yay. If they won't, take lots of photos. Repurpose it.

If you're a guest on someone's show, sometimes you can co-create it and post it on both of your podcasts. Two birds with one stone. At the very least, if they give you the video, you can make reels out of it.

If you do a workshop, have your team break it all up and put it on social media.

I follow an entrepreneur who is a leader in the Instagram space. He teaches people how to use Instagram for their businesses. A good two-thirds of his posts are repurposed. He takes it, tweaks it, puts it back. (No, his *team* does.) And nobody knows. I know, because I'm a student of business, and I'm studying him really closely. But nobody else really knows—or cares.

Everything you produce is a seed. Everything. How can you make a forest out of it by repurposing it over and over again?

One of the biggest objections I hear about starting a podcast or a YouTube channel (besides fear) is: "I don't have the time." It doesn't have to take as much time as you imagine it will. Just because I'm visible on social media a lot doesn't mean I'm actually spending time there. You can do this too. People will think you're everywhere. And you will be, but it's not going to take you a lot of time like people assume. One and done.

I'm telling you: repurposing is magic.

Leverage These Three Things to Build Your System

If you can master batching, delegation, and repurposing, you've found the keys to building your dream business and living your dream life. You can build a system where you do these things once and hand them off to your team that takes them, runs with them, and repurposes them.

Just like everything else we talk about, it's so simple. But, if you're committed to it, it will change your business and your life.

Some Important Reminders

I am a student of businesses that grow really big and stand the test of time. They survive in the good times, and they survive in the bad times. That's because they stick to principles and strategies that are classics. They always work.

Whatever your dream for your business is, whatever your goal is, I want you to hear me very clearly: these are the best things you can do for your business. Stay focused, so you can become known for what you do.

There are people who, when I look at their social media, I cannot tell what they do. I have the opportunity to refer a lot of business to them and help them cross every revenue goal they have, but I can't tell what they do, so I can't refer to them.

You've got to be clear. We live in an attention economy. Everybody's going for everybody's attention. You've got to cut through the noise.

When building an HQ feels overwhelming, remember why you're doing it. You don't want to be someone who goes to speak somewhere and people hear you and love you and go to find you online and you're nowhere. You want them to Google you, and this beautiful body of work shows up. They binge it, and then they want to work with you.

And when going to other people's audiences feels scary, remember why you're doing it. You don't want to be the world's best-kept secret. It's not enough to post on your own social media platforms. People aren't just going to find you. You have to go to where they are. You can't hide behind your computer and stay in your own little world.

You've got to go out there. And if you're an introvert, I feel you, but so am I. You can't have an excuse, because I exist. I can show you the way, but you don't have an excuse. Now, they're gonna find you, and they're gonna come back. And just like they do on Netflix, they're going to want to binge. So make that commitment to go find them.

When you're worried that your HQ isn't perfect, remember that perfection is not required. I started my podcast with an iPhone 7. It's now a top 1% podcast by global rankings. Perfection isn't the goal. Do your best and keep getting better and better.

Batching, delegating, and repurposing are going to save us time and help us build successful businesses simultaneously. You're building something that, the bigger it gets, the bigger and better your life gets. Remember, I have no interest in building a business that robs me of my life.

Ironically, I've had people tell me they really want to join EntreMD Business School but they just don't have the time. One of the big things we learn in EBS is how to make time for our business. You won't just magically "find" time lying around. There are practices and skills you learn—the CEO calendar, the 80/20 rule, time blocking, etc.—to help you do things smarter so you free up more time. One of the biggest takeaways from EBS is that we get more done—and have more fun—in less time.

We have a doctor in EBS who recently had a family emergency. And she was able to walk away from her business—no harm, no foul— and took care of what she needed to take care of. She's actually done that twice now.

Another doctor is running a very successful practice, and he gets home at 4:00pm every day to be with his kids. Another doctor is running a million dollar practice, and they decided they're taking three months off and are going to Mexico.

We don't have to believe the lie that private practice is dead and physicians can't be entrepreneurs. As a community, let's decide to stop rolling over and playing dead.

We're going to build businesses that work. We're going to build businesses that can compete on any stage. In EBS, I end every call the same way: we are the people building the most innovative, most impactful, most profitable businesses. And we can compete with any entrepreneur on any stage. We don't believe the lie anymore. This is our time.

Are you with me?

If you haven't already, head over to www.entremd. com/visiblitybook to download your workbook. Radical transformation begins here.

EBS Student Spotlight: Dr. Funke Afolabi-Brown

Dr. Funke Afolabi-Brown owns a company called Restful Sleep MD. Her mission is to empower busy women and their children to prioritize sleep. She does this through speaking, consultation, coaching and more recently through her private practice.

She says that, two years ago, "before EBS happened to me," she had no clue. All she knew was that she was uncomfortable and restless. "I was just like, 'Wait, is this it?'" She was working in an academic institution—and publishing and mentoring—and was very successful. "I was doing the things I thought were 'it' for me, but it just didn't feel like it."

She didn't really have a business idea and had never done any coaching or anything like it, but she started listening to the EntreMD podcast and "Honestly, that really started opening my eyes regarding possibilities." She knew she needed to get into the community, because all of the free resources had already changed her mindset in an incredible way.

She was employed full time, but she started working on her brand. She began blogging. "I was just kind of trying to put myself out there," she says, "applying the things I was learning. And so I jumped right in and, slowly but surely, I got a sense of what my business idea was and started implementing things, putting myself out there, and really getting better at it."

She stresses that it wasn't perfect, and she doesn't believe in waiting until you have it all figured out before you get started. "My mission when I started was different from now," she says, "and it keeps evolving. We just keep reiterating, listening to what our clients want, and moving forward with it. It's been a life-changing experience."

She says there's work involved and you have to be committed to that work. "Things don't just happen because you're in the community. You leverage the community to do the work that you have the potential to do."

She has also learned a lot about herself. "My confidence has grown as a physician who also has a business—which, I really didn't think I could put those two words together before EBS, so the mindset shift has been huge. And also just the ability, the potential to dream."

She was talking to a colleague recently who said she felt stuck and tired, so tired she doesn't even have the space to think of what she wants to do next. Dr. Funke told her, "There's hope for you!" And she went on to talk her through some things she had learned in EBS and let her know she has options. She doesn't have to stay stuck. "I was inspired just hearing myself speak to her," she says. "Being able to encourage others has been incredible."

Dr. Funke recently left her paid employment to go fully in with her business. "It took a while getting there," she says, "But I'm so happy I made that decision. I'm very excited. I'm not saying everyone has to leave their job. I just knew I was ready to make that shift."

A lot of what she does involves coaching women and children—and consultations and speaking. She's also been a guest on close to 75 podcasts. "I'm like hardcore," she says. "I don't do 100% of what Dr. Una says, but I try.."

Initially she said yes to every opportunity that came up, but now she's recognizing that she has a skill set and deserves to get paid well to speak. "It's helping me set boundaries and choose the opportunities," she says. "It's helping me learn to ask and really master my call to action. I tell people, 'I will speak to your organization on how you can use sleep as a superpower to enhance productivity.' I tell women to come work with me so they can get their energy back by getting their sleep on track."

She says she consistently puts herself out there. She'll be paid to speak on a stage, and when she steps off, people will reach out and say, "Hey, here's our card. We want you to come speak to our organization."

She believes the sky's the limit. "I think we're the only ones that can limit how far we can go when we really explore that entrepreneurial side of us," she says. She credits the non-judgmental EBS community with helping her get this far. It's such a positive and generous community and she knows people have her back. "It's been more than worth its weight in gold in terms of the return on investment in my mindset—and the tangibles as well."

Dr. Funke was just featured on ABC which was a huge deal. "People have bombarded my website and started reaching out," she says, "and it's been incredible. Nothing like this would have been possible if not for the business school and me really putting myself out there. They found me because I was googleable, and it was just such a delight.

So many opportunities have opened up to her. "And I know it's just the beginning," she says. "The snowball is coming."

CHAPTER 5:

Next Steps

I've said over and over again that we physicians had a dream when we went to medical school. Our dream was to help people. And, in these wild and crazy times, that dream has turned into a nightmare. Why? Because we don't have freedom. We're controlled. We can't practice medicine how we want. We can't make a living how we want. We can't have the life we want. We've lost our autonomy; we're burned out. And many of us are ready to give up.

But there is a way, a vehicle, to get back to your dream.

That vehicle is entrepreneurship, and that is what the EntreMD Business School is all about. EBS is the #1 business school for physician entrepreneurs who want to build 6-, 7-, and multiple 7-figure businesses. It's a year-long program exclusively for physicians and the only school of its kind. You get the coaching, the accountability, the community—everything you need to build a successful thriving business.

We were told to stay in your lane; take care of the patients; we'll take care of everything else. That has not worked for us. So we need to take care of everything else too. And we can.

Don't believe the lie that doctors don't know business. I know from experience that physicians actually make some of the best entrepreneurs. We put people and service before profit. In EBS, you'll learn how to add the profit element, so you can serve *and* earn. This is what gives us financial freedom.

I'm here to tell you that you can live life and practice medicine on your terms.

It's Not a Cost; It's an Investment

Your tuition for EBS is an investment, not a cost. It's officially a one-year program, but we have people in their fourth year who just keep killing it in bigger dimensions. I want to tell you how to get the most out of your year (or more if you choose to keep going). The tagline, when I created the school, was: *the only school you'll never want to graduate from.* In true EBS fashion, we have people who have been here for four years. They never want to leave, and we don't make them. They even created their own hashtag, #EBSforlife.

If you were to go to Emory University in Atlanta to get an MBA, it's $70k a year. Most MBA programs tell you that the average graduate of their program gets a job with a salary of $150k or $180k. But we're not here trying to learn business to get a job. We're here to start and run our own businesses.

We want to be entrepreneurs.

We do not call it a cost, because it's not a cost. Just like investing in real estate is not a cost; it's an investment. And, if you show up with the attitude of "I'm going to get a return on my investment," that's exactly what you're going to get. We'll show you how to create wins so big that you'll say, "The EntreMD Business School was the best investment I made in my life and in my business."

One doctor said, "When I heard about the investment, I gulped." But then she did the math. "If I could serve x number of clients over the course of a year, I'd make my money back." And so she made that mental switch from cost to investment. She invested in herself, established herself as a thought leader, and has a lot of wins under her belt and many more coming.

You're not throwing away your money. You're investing it and expecting a return.

I had my own "gulp moment" at an event in 2017 where they told me about a mastermind that sounded amazing. Then I found out it was $43,000. My initial reaction was "no way." Then I said to myself, "You know what? You've watched these guys deliver at a high level. You've experienced transformation just from their free stuff. What would it be like to work with them for 10 months?" I gulped really big, and then I signed up for it. My husband and I still talk about it being the best $43,000 we've ever spent.

I can guarantee that, if you're committed to your goals, and you're coachable, and you will stay in conversation, your investment in EBS will be the best money you've ever spent. And that's the truth. I hope, like me, you'll gulp really loud and then say yes to yourself.

We have had over 250 physicians enroll in the EntreMD Business School. We've studied what makes people succeed in EBS, and I'll give you the exact blueprint so you can succeed too.

I have never lost money on a program, including the programs that were not the right fit for me, because I walked in as a savvy entrepreneur and said, "I'm going to make my money back." And I always do.

The EntreMD Business School is a container, a carefully curated environment where you can thrive and implement everything you've just learned in community with other physician entrepreneurs who are doing the exact same things in their own businesses. In building the EntreMD Business School, we built an incubator and an accelerator that you can put doctors in and it will pull out all the greatness you have inside of you—your ideas, goals, and big dreams.

Dreams come true in EBS. They really do. I built exactly what I wish I would have had back when I started on my entrepreneurial journey. I incorporated all the elements that helped me thrive and grow my businesses to what they are today.

So let's talk about how to 10x your investment. And bear in mind that this is me being exceptionally conservative, because we've got students in the school who have done way more. How can you take that investment and turn it into a return?

I love it when people tell me that they made such a huge return on their investment in the EntreMD Business School that they owe me. I say, "That's okay, you can keep it."

Five Simple but Important Steps to 10xing Your Investment

The first step in 10xing your investment is: **make a decision**. You decide it. You declare it. "I'm going to 10x my investment. This is going to be the best investment I've ever made in my business." I cannot tell you how powerful making a decision is.

Sometimes we hold off on making that decision because of fear. "Now I have to live up to it. I have to do the work."

The second step: **commit to doing the work**. If you don't want to work, then being an entrepreneur will be painful for you. Now, I'm all for working smarter, but even smart work is hard work. That said, I will help make things simpler and get you results faster. But entrepreneurship isn't about passive income; it's an active sport.

When I talk about hard work, I'm not talking about your life being completely out of balance and neglecting your family. In EBS, one of our core values is building your dream business and your dream life *at the same time*. But it's hard work. And fun work. And we'll help you work on the 20% that actually matters, the 20% that will get you to your dreams faster. But you've got to commit to doing the work.

If you do the hard work up front, you can rest even more later. Progressively, you can increase your amount of rest. In December 2021, I decided I wanted to take a sabbatical from my private practice. I did a lot of work up to that point, so I could take an extended time of rest. Of course, I'm still hard at work on my businesses—especially EntreMD.

The third step: **redefine your relationship with failure**. This is especially important for us physicians. If you are a neurosurgeon or a heart surgeon or a pediatrician putting a needle in a newborn's spinal column, I want you to aim for perfection.

But, in business, you are going to fail a lot in order to succeed a lot. But it's not fatal. It doesn't make you a failure. It's like you tested something in the lab. It's like you're learning to put in IVs. You don't try it once and quit. Failure is just part of the process.

Winston Churchill defined success as going from failure to failure without losing your enthusiasm. Remember that and you'll enjoy your entrepreneurial journey. You will have the opportunity to act on a lot of new concepts in the EntreMD Business School, and some of them don't work. We figure out what went wrong and either tweak it or try something different. Ask questions in the EBS Facebook group and get feedback from your fellow entrepreneurs.

And when we talk about failure, we're not talking about *you* as a failure. You're not a failure. You're in the ring, getting stuff done, doing the work, being the leader. I have an unbelievable amount of respect for physician entrepreneurs. You're a visionary, a trailblazer. You're setting the stage and changing the narrative for the physician community.

People are so open and vulnerable in this group, and it pays off for them in huge ways. Somebody will come in and say, "I did a webinar, it didn't go according to plan. I only got half as many people as I'd hoped." And they'll do a full debrief. Listening to somebody talk through their "failed project" is a whole masterclass.

Why do so many businesses fail in the first year? Because people haven't redefined their relationship with failure. With the right attitude toward failure, you will crush it. You will fly.

Step 4: **trade comparison for inspiration**. I'm a part of communities where someone might say, "I'm really happy about the direction our business is going in. We're doing an easy million a month." *A million? Easy? A month?" All in one sentence?* When I hear something like this, I have a couple options. I can choose to compare and get discouraged and think my business sucks—or I can be inspired. That's my choice.

When I hear someone say that the valuation of their business is $500 million, I have a choice. You can compare yourself to others, go into hiding, and say, "I don't belong here because everybody's better than me," or you can choose to be curious, be inspired to go after your big dreams.

Decide you're going to be curious and inspired. You belong here. When you join the EntreMD Business School, you're going to meet all kinds of people. People who just gave their third TED Talk. People who just got paid $20k to give a talk. People who just completed their first year in private practice and crossed the million dollar mark. People whose businesses grew by $2.5 million in a year.

You literally get to see behind the scenes of hugely successful businesses. You'll see wins that could intimidate you or inspire you—but you get to choose. And you know what? You're an amazing person too. Show up like you belong here, and choose to be inspired.

Your network is your net worth. When you join the EntreMD Business School, your net worth just explodes. Why? Because now you're in a diverse community of physician entrepreneurs who are actively growing all kinds of businesses. We're not doing cookie cutter here. We intentionally provide you with a broader range of experiences, connections, and ideas. Innovation isn't always something that's brand new. Innovation can be taking something that's a known principle in one industry and bringing it to your industry. It's a very diverse group on purpose. Our group is the happiest place on earth for physicians (their words, not mine). To be honest with you, the EntreMD private network is worth the tuition of the school. Just the network. Just the people. Leverage it.

How do all the businesses thrive in one container? Because we help you build a business *system*. No matter what type of business you have, you're going to have to understand numbers, run a meeting, build a team, figure out the marketing and sales and how to create repeat customers. You need the mindset of a physician entrepreneur.

Forget comparison. Choose inspiration and curiosity instead. Show up. Be your whole self. And believe you belong here. Because you do. Celebrate others. Your turn will come.

Step 5: **engage in all the elements of the school**. When EBS started in 2020, we only had the Wednesday calls and the Facebook group. Every year, we've listened to what people needed and wanted and added different elements to help them get results faster and more consistently. Everything is designed on purpose to solve a specific problem.

EBS is not like medical school. You don't need 100% attendance but you have to engage as much as you can for your stage of life and business to get everything you need out of it. We take the most classic principles that have always worked and will always work, and make you experts at that. And we don't say "this is the one prescribed way of doing everything," because there are all kinds of different businesses. We show you how to think and take strategic action like ultra successful entrepreneurs.

Our private Facebook community is an interactive environment—an incubator—where you can give help, receive help, acknowledge your wins, share your trials, network with people, connect people to others, get connected to others. The network is mind-blowingly powerful. It's so rich we call it the EBS Commonwealth. If you take advantage of it, it will really turn everything around for you.

To summarize, take these five simple steps:

1. Make a decision.
2. Commit to doing the work.
3. Redefine your relationship to failure.
4. Trade comparison for inspiration.
5. Engage in all the elements of the school.

And you'll set yourself up to 10x your investment in EBS. The only person who does not do well in EBS is a person who doesn't want to learn or do the work. If you're willing to learn and do the work, you're golden. Your job is to invest, take these steps, keep your eyes on the prize, and do the work to get that prize.

Climb Onto the Rocket Ship

Dr. Kirin Palmer listened to the EntreMD podcast for three months, then joined EBS and gained the confidence she needed to launch her own practice. She had patients knocking on her door before she even opened, and four months in, her practice was already profitable. She says the accountability in EBS played a big part in that. She got comfortable being uncomfortable and pushed herself farther than she thought she could go.

"Like Dr. Una says, the more you lean into it, the more you get back," she says. "If you have a business or want to start one, EBS is the place to be. It's like an enzyme catalyst to a chemical reaction."

She could have read books and listened to podcasts forever, she said, but being with a group of physicians in EBS is "like being on a rocket ship. It's the best investment I've ever made in my business and even in myself. It's been an incredible ride and I think I'll probably be an EBS-for-lifer."

When you're part of EBS, it transforms you as a human, as a physician, and as an entrepreneur. You no longer fit in a box. You'll hardly recognize yourself—in the very best way.

"Every month I get my investment back—" Dr. Kirin says, "either in saving money because of the business decision I made or a tip I got from another EBS classmate. It's an investment that pays for itself very quickly. And if you really want to create the masterpiece of your life, this is the way to do it. I've been able to craft a practice with flexible scheduling that really reflects who I am as a physician and my returning patients absolutely love it."

One of the things we say in the EntreMD Business School is "the greatest reward of building a business is not the business." The greatest reward is who you become. The best investment you can make is the one in yourself.

The EBS Framework

The EBS experience is nearly impossible to describe until you're inside. But I can give you a peek into what the container looks like. We call it The EBS Framework:

- Weekly live sessions (every Wed at 7pm)
- Monthly momentum challenges (a revenue generating sprint)
- Private facebook community (worth the price tag alone)
- Weekly CEO power hour (a coworking space)
- Specialty in-person masterminds and retreats
- EBS vault (includes every training from 2020 on)
- EBS Book Club

I wish I could take you on a tour of the EBS Facebook group, but it's a sacred place you can only access when you make the commitment to join. People ask questions. Big ones, small ones. Basic questions, high-level questions. Everyone is so generous with their answers. And you don't ever have to be afraid to ask something.

I share a lot of personal information and numbers about my business. I truly believe that I'm a vision board for the EBS students in the sense that I am living my life out loud. I want doctors to see what I'm doing and say, "Wait, that's possible? I had no idea."

In 2021, I set a goal to do a million dollars in revenue, so doctors can believe they can do it too. The second we hit $1M, I told the students in the Facebook group, "This is how we did it." I literally took them behind the scenes, showed them how we figured out the strategy, what we implemented, the roadblocks, the mistakes we made. That's what happens in that community.

We have a retreat in October and a business makeover mastermind in April. If you can imagine the goodness that's happening in the private Facebook group, imagine what happens when we all get together in person. Pure magic.

The EBS Vault is filled with every single training that has ever been done in the EntreMD Business School since its inception in 2020. It's like liquid gold. I have people who are in their third year in the EntreMD Business School who are going back and watching those trainings and are like, "This is so good. It's hitting differently now."

The EBS community has been described as an alternate reality where people have a completely different experience than they've ever had. Your dreams don't get knocked. When you need help, people come out of the woodwork to help you and support you. It has been such a joy. When you hear about the wins, it's not just business wins. It's family, it's health, spirituality — wins in every single area of life.

Make a Definitive Decision TODAY

You have three options right now. Your radical transformation is at the mercy of your decision.

You might be thinking, "Dr. Una, this book was awesome. You rock. You gave us your best stuff. I've got it, and I'm going to run with it on my own." That's Option #1. I support you, and I'll celebrate your wins with you.

Option #2: do nothing. Please don't choose this option. Don't do nothing.

Option #3: you can fasttrack this. People are your shortcut to success. For everything you're trying to do in business, someone has been there before. They've already done it. They've gone to the school of hard knocks, make the mistakes, and learned the lessons. With the right coaching and community, you can shave years off your learning curve.

If that's you, your next step is to head over to www. entremd.com/business to schedule a call with my team.

We have no interest in strong-arming anyone to join EBS. We only want people to join who are a good fit. We want people who are committed and coachable.

I end our EBS sessions with "Don't forget who you are." You are the ones building the most innovative, most impactful, most profitable businesses. Whatever we're doing, we're not building status quo businesses. We're done with the way things have always been done.

I have a private practice, an education business (EntreMD), a marketing agency, and a non-profit. All four need business systems. I want to spend my time serving doctors. Because I've built a business system, I have the freedom to do that.

We had a doctor in EBS who said, "I'm gonna make a million dollars." She had no idea how it was going to happen. But she sent me a private message three days ago that said, "Dr. Una, a million dollars. We crossed it."

In five years, what we're doing now will be normalized. The people who've already joined EBS are early adopters. They're the ones who will set the stage for what is going to come and they're going to lead the charge—and I want you to be one of them.

And it doesn't end with building a successful business. Once you build a successful business, you'll have money to invest, which will help you build an empire and leave a legacy.

I cannot wait to serve and support you, I cannot wait for you to meet the other docs in the school.

Every time we share stories from physicians in EBS, people tell me, "That's amazing, but that's not me. I'm not that good. I couldn't do that." And here's what I need you to know: unicorns are not born; they're made. When doctors share their stories, they're always so generous to take us back to the beginning with all their doubts and fears. But they all dared their fears and said yes. And now they're on the other side of that.

One of our physicians told me recently, "Thank you, Dr. Una and my EBS tribe, for surrounding me with examples of what is possible. Let's make a herd of unicorns and start a stampede in the doctor world."

You will thrive here. You will excel here. You'll be one of those people whose stories I share. You'll be blown away. You'll say, "I don't recognize myself anymore. I don't know who this person is." That will be your story as you build your dream business and your dream life.

Come join the EBS Commonwealth today!

www.entremd.com/business

Acknowledgments

I want to thank the following special people:

Makeda Omensa who runs so much behind the scenes in all my businesses and in my life. Thank you for doing all you do so I have the freedom to live nine lives at once.

Natalie Delamater with the Physician's Marketing Team who is the creative genius behind the visual elements and technology of my multiple-seven figure brands. Thank you for bringing every one of my visions to life.

Fatima Sparks, my practice administrator who has led our practice through a pandemic, the great resignation and hyperinflation. Without your work, I would not be free to change the lives of tens of thousands of physicians.

The physicians of the EntreMD Business School. You are the ones building the most innovative, most impactful and most profitable businesses inside and outside healthcare. Working with you is one of the greatest honors of my life. I am grateful for you beyond words.

My four children, Cheta, Chidi, Chichi and Esther. I love you so much and I am so proud of you. Thank you for inspiring me every day to be the best version of myself.

CONNECT WITH THE AUTHOR

 www.entremd.com

 @DrUnachukwu

 @DrUnachukwu

 EntreMD - Physicians in Business

 @DrUna

Nneka Unachukwu, MD
Pediatrician, Best-Selling Author & CEO

ADDITIONAL RESOURCES

The EntreMD Podcast

Dr. Una is passionate about helping physicians embrace entrepreneurship so they can have the financial freedom to live life and practice medicine on their own terms.

 entremd.com/podcast

Dr. Una on YouTube

Subscribe to Dr. Una's YouTube channel for insightful interviews, inspirational success stories, and expert business, marketing and branding tips.

 @drunachukwu

MORE BOOKS FROM THE AUTHOR

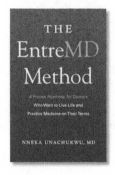

Not everyone can do what it takes to become a doctor—but you did. From graduating medical school to completing your residency, each step has gotten you closer to living the life you've envisioned since first completing that med school application.

But are you living the life you want?

You signed up to save lives and help change the world, not to build a brand and become an entrepreneur. Still, to succeed, you need a plan for navigating the business of your profession. In *The EntreMD Method*, pediatrician and entrepreneur Nneka Unachukwu provides a roadmap for strategizing your business and building a successful brand that reflects your goals. Whether you're interested in coaching and consulting, running a product-based business, starting a nonprofit, or opening a private practice, leveraging proven sales and marketing practices will help lay the financial foundation you need. Learn how to tackle this next challenge head-on and take control of your life with Dr. Una's roadmap for living life on your terms.

When Dr. Nneka Unachukwu started her practice in 2010, there were no coaching programs, podcasts, or YouTube channels around to teach her how to be a physician entrepreneur. She had some resources, but what she really wanted was to meet with people like her.

Made for More is the peer resource Dr. Unachukwu wishes she'd had. With stories from over forty doctors from the EntreMD Business School, see how these physician entrepreneurs overcame fear, self-doubt, lack of experience, and other obstacles to create success on their terms. Follow their journeys to thriving physician entrepreneurship through endeavors such as building their brands and starting private practices, coaching practices, and nonprofits.

It's normal to want more. Let the stories within open your eyes to new possibilities and teach you practical steps you can take to start your journey to more.

Available at entremd.com/books

About the Author

D r. Nneka Unachukwu helps physicians build profitable 7 and 7+ figure businesses by teaching them the simple, proven and timeless principles used by the ultra successful. She knows that entrepreneurship is a vehicle physicians can leverage so they can have the freedom to live life and practice medicine on their terms. She does this through the EntreMD Business School, the only school of its kind for physician entrepreneurs, the EntreMD podcast, a top 10 podcast, and her best-selling books.

Before starting EntreMD, Dr. Una started her own pediatric private practice, a practice she still runs fourteen years later. In her typical unconventional fashion, she built it as a true business, one that can run efficiently and profitably without her involvement in the day-to-day management.

Dr. Una has been featured in *Forbes* and her company hit #315 on the Inc. 5000 list of fastest-growing privately held companies in America in 2023.

She resides outside Atlanta with her husband and four children.

Made in the USA
Las Vegas, NV
19 June 2024

91250958R00090